The Sex Trafficker's Wife

A Story of Truth, Faith, and Trust in Self

A. Quick

Green Heart Living Press

The Sex Trafficker's Wife: A Story of Truth, Faith, and Trust in Self

ISBN Paperback: 978-1-954493-38-4

Cover design: Barb Pritchard, Infinity Brand Designs

GREEN HEART
LIVING
— PRESS —

Dedication

This story is dedicated to all those still fighting to create safety in their lives and the lives of their children.

Acknowledgments

I have been blessed by so much support from those around me throughout this journey.

I want to start by thanking my three children, my greatest teachers. They have shown me time and time again how much more I was capable of. You are such amazing humans and I cannot wait to see what you create in the world.

To my mom, step-dad, and sister, thank you for always supporting me. I wasn't always able to hear you, but you never gave up. Special thanks to you mom for always jumping in to help me in any way you can, including helping me to edit this book.

To Mark, thank you for teaching me how to have fun again when I truly needed it the most.

To all of my friends and co-workers who listened and held space for me through the endlessly frustrating times—thank you so much.

To every friend who took the extra step to introduce me to someone who might be able to help me with my case, thank you. That support, those contacts, changed everything.

To my legal team at Anderson & Baker, you guys are the best of the best. I could not have asked for a more dedicated support team. Curtis, you are a rock star.

To Melinda, you went above and beyond to help me accurately represent the facts of the case. I am so grateful for your integrity and support.

To Liv, thank you for seeing me and supporting me through the hardest time in my life. Thank you for helping me never give up and suggesting avenues outside of the traditional therapy box.

To my dear friend Brittany, thank you for getting me back on track to finish writing this book.

To my husband Justin, thank you for teaching me and my children what it means to be truly safe in a man's arms.

To my editor Liz, and the entire team at Green Heart Press, you guys are freaking amazing at what you do!

And to Charlie, whether you ever read this book or not, it's important for me to say that after all that happened I am immensely grateful to you. I can finally say and really mean it, I forgive you. I have learned so much, and grown so much, and without this experience I could never be where I am today. From the bottom of my heart, thank you for the final gift of peace that you gave to me and to the boys.

Introduction

Everything in this book happened exactly as I wrote it to the best of my ability.

Names of my children, friends, and family have all been changed out of respect for those who do not yet wish to have their stories told.

The name of my now ex-husband has not been changed out of respect for the truth of my experience. My relationship was real and valid and his crime and the facts of our divorce are public record. Everything I share in this book is from my own perspective.

My goal in writing this book is not to create a chorus of people telling me I was brave, or strong, or whatever other applause they choose to insert here.

My goal in writing this book is to reach out to everyone who is struggling. To let them know they are not alone.

To every parent who is sharing custody with their abuser, you are not alone.

To every parent who is sharing custody with their child's abuser, you are not alone.

To every person who is in a relationship that they are not emotionally, psychologically, physically, or sexually safe in, you are not alone.

To every parent who is barely making ends meet, and unable to financially invest in the fight to protect your children, you are not alone.

To every person who is sitting in their trauma, unable to see a way forward, to know what to do to fix it, you are not alone.

To everyone who reads this and resonates with any part of my story, you, too, are not alone.

My goal in writing this is to inspire every one of you

to seek change, to make the bold choices for yourself and for your children in spite of the fear.

It's time we all stand in our power and our truth and claim our place in this world.

With Love,
Amanda

Chapter 1

It was a Tuesday in late April of 2016. Ethan, my oldest son, was turning six in just a couple of days, and Axel had just turned four. Milo, my baby, was only 14 months old and still nursing quite frequently. It seemed like most days, he was literally attached to me 24/7. He was either directly on my breast or wrapped up in a baby carrier on my back. My three boys were my whole world.

My mom was on her way to visit us in Colorado from where she lived in Hawaii. She tried to visit at least annually and usually came during the two big boys' birthday week at the end of April. I was feeling the pressure to make sure I got everything ready in time. My relationship with my mom hadn't been so great, really, since I was a teenager, which is why I moved out at 17. She wanted to connect with me, but I wasn't super interested. She could be passive-aggressive, and I had always felt she had so many expectations of who I was supposed to turn out to be, and clearly, I wasn't meeting them.

Thankfully, I had scheduled a house cleaner to come help me get ready. When I was pregnant with Milo, I finally hired someone to help out every couple of weeks. Charlie, my husband, had been getting upset that I didn't keep the house clean enough. He did eventually realize that he, too, was capable of cleaning, but instead of doing so, he suggested I hire someone. Keeping the house picture-perfect clean was near impossible with three kids under five, but that was my job those days, the house and the kids.

Before I had my kids, I had a career. I had worked in the information technology field since I was 17, and I was

pretty darn good at it. Puzzles and technology just came easily to me. After I had Ethan, I quit my job to stay home full-time. The pull to take care of my babies was stronger than I ever could have imagined. Leaving them in the care of strangers never felt like a viable choice for me. I was grateful for the financial support from Charlie's job which allowed me to stay home with the boys. Most days, I was happy with that choice. I felt guilty that I wasn't contributing money to our budget as I'd always been ultra-independent—but I knew that babyhood was short, and things would shift and change over time.

On that day in April, Charlie left for work around seven am, which was his usual time. He generally didn't even wake us when he left. He worked long hours most days—out the door by seven am and not home till seven or eight at night. I expected him home even later that evening as his mom had asked for help getting some old bikes out of her garage. His dad had passed away the December before, and she had been working on clearing out his old stuff.

The day itself was normal. The big kids had kindergarten and preschool, and I ran my errands. Milo was still taking two naps a day, and I usually lay down with him for at least one of them. He had me up two or three times a night nursing and so catching up on sleep was important on the days the boys had school.

That evening I put the kids down for bed at about eight pm. I went downstairs, watched some TV, and waited for Charlie to be home. He sent me a text around nine pm asking if there were any leftovers for dinner. I responded, "yes." His mom's house was only about 15 minutes away, so I assumed that meant he was just on his way home.

Thirty minutes passed, then an hour. I called his cell phone. It rang once and went straight to voicemail. The next try went straight to voicemail. I tried a few more

times, confused. I decided to call and check in with his mom before it got any later. Maybe he was still there? She was surprised to hear from me this late—he had left over an hour ago. Well, then where the hell did he go? Maybe he decided to pick up food after all? She thought maybe he'd decided to just go drop the bikes off on his way home.

It was not an unusual occurrence for Charlie to turn off his phone or not respond. In fact, ever since I left my day job and became a full-time stay-at-home parent, he was so much less reachable to me. If I called at five pm asking when he would be home from work so we could have a family dinner together, I would get told "soon"— only for him to show up long after the kids were in bed. If I asked him to please come home sooner, I was told he was doing the best he could. I felt guilty enough that he was financially providing for us, and so I did not dare to question the commitment he had. If I got angry or frustrated, I would be met with defensiveness. I tried every communication trick I could think of over the years. I eventually stopped calling entirely and stopped asking. It was easier not to get worked up and I just figured he'd show up when he showed. Nothing I did ever changed this pattern.

So not being able to reach him that night was not unusual. I just assumed he had gotten caught up in something and didn't want me to bother him. I turned off the TV and decided to go to bed. I fully expected him to stroll in any minute, but I was not wasting sleep over it.

I woke up at two am when Milo started fussing to nurse. I snuggled and nursed him back to sleep and tried to listen to see if Charlie was home. I assumed he had to be here by now, but something in me wasn't certain. Once Milo finished, I ninja-rolled out of the bed so I wouldn't disturb him and went to check downstairs. Charlie and I hadn't slept in the same bed since Ethan

was a little baby. He just seemed to prefer the couch and falling asleep to the TV over sharing a bed with me and the current nursling. I hated the TV noise and preferred silence or simple white noise. It worked for us. And with three kids, it clearly didn't prevent us from being intimate.

I peeked downstairs—no Charlie. I checked outside. The van he had taken that morning to ferry the bikes—that wasn't home either. His phone still went straight to voicemail. *What the fuck? Where was he?* I went back to bed not wanting Milo to wake and realize I was gone. If he woke, and I wasn't there he'd squeal so loud the other two would wake up too. So, I just laid there trying to stay calm. My mind was racing. *Where could he be?* I mean, he was notoriously late, sure, but not this late. He'd never done this before. My mind immediately went to a worst-case scenario. *Was he dead in a ditch somewhere? What if he was actually gone? I was going to be all alone with three kids—oh my god the boys! How was I going to support us? That man was their father, and the love of my life.* I shoved that thought out of my mind. That couldn't be it, but I had to figure out what was happening.

I got up again and snuck into the kitchen so the boys wouldn't hear me. This time I called the hospital. Maybe they have him and they just haven't been able to call me. They answered and checked the admission records. No Charlie. And no John Does either.

Back to bed again I went. Where is he? I fell back asleep for a short while and woke up again to Milo rooting for the boob. I nursed him again, making sure he was all the way back asleep before sneaking out again. It was now five am.

I paced around the house. I tried his cell again—straight to voice mail. Who else could I call at this hour? I couldn't exactly go looking for him. I had three kids asleep in the house. I then had the idea to try calling

non-emergency dispatch. The TV makes it seem like a person has to be missing for 24 hours but maybe there was something they could do now. I called. The lady who answered listened to me explain what had happened. My husband hadn't come home last night, and this was so unlike him, could she help? She said she was going to transfer me to the jail first to see if he was there. "Oh, well OK," I said. I thought that was very unlikely, but whatever. She said to call her back if he wasn't there and she could help. "OK, thank you. I'll call you right back."

Another lady answered at the jail. I told her I was looking for my husband and gave her his name.

She replied, "Yeah, we have him."

"WHAT? You *have* him? Charles Watts? Really? On what charge? How much to bail him out?" I was so confused.

This made no sense.

What she said next was perhaps the last thing I ever expected to hear come out of anyone's mouth.

The charge was *Attempted Human Trafficking*, and his bond was *250 thousand dollars*. If I had cash, I could bail him out anytime.

I nearly dropped the phone. *WHAT? Wait WHAT?* I couldn't even think straight. I wanted to ask more questions. But I didn't even know where to start. I thanked her and hung up the phone.

I was now wide awake. I started googling like crazy. What does that charge even mean? Human trafficking was what, like stealing people and moving them across borders? Like in shipping containers? To *sell them?* It made exactly zero sense to me. It could not be possible that Charlie was involved in something like this. He was a father, husband, and had a good job. We were comfortable. Hell, I technically had access to enough cash to bail him out right now.

I found numbers for a bail bondsman. I called and to

my surprise they picked up the phone at 5:30 am. The man I spoke to was very helpful and explained how this process worked. For 10 percent down and a lean on the house, they could help bail him out today. But he also said that there would be a bond hearing in a day or two and most of the time these types of charges were reduced down to $100,000, so it was possibly worth waiting a few more hours. He offered to go check on Charlie for me at the jail once they opened, which I accepted. I was so grateful. I needed someone to get eyes on him. Part of me thought maybe someone just had his wallet somehow and it wasn't going to actually be him. But if that wasn't him, then I still didn't know where he was.

I hung up and started trying to call lawyers. I've certainly watched enough crime shows to know that I needed a lawyer ASAP. I left a bunch of messages for everyone I could find on google. Durango, Colorado was a pretty small town, and so there were only two or three that looked promising for criminal cases.

It was now closer to seven am. The boys would be up soon. I really didn't want to wake them early. They'd be impossible to get back down at this point. I tried to stay quiet and not pace around too much.

My phone rang and it was one of the lawyer's offices calling me back. Wow, he was at work early, but hey, that was awesome. He listened to me and repeated much of what the bail bondsman said: bond hearing tomorrow or the next day and there was an almost guaranteed reduction in the amount. He also said he could see me today at 11 am in his office. "Perfect, I'll be there."

I then called Charlie's mom knowing she'd be up by now. I told her that he never did come home but I had found him in jail. I told her the charge and what I knew so far. She said she was coming right over. She also suggested I try to get Axel in preschool today. It was normally just Ethan's day to attend kindergarten, but not

14

having to worry about Axel today would be super helpful. She wanted to go straight to the jail to try to see him as soon as they opened.

The boys started waking up. I made coffee for myself and breakfast for them. The school agreed Axel could come in today. I told them it was a family emergency hoping that was enough to not have to answer any more questions. *Good, OK.* We had a sort of plan. Next steps at least.

Charlie's mom arrived and we packed up the boys to take them to school. We were going to drop them off and then head straight to the jail. I ran inside and checked them in. The car ride was tense. We were both so confused. She kept talking about the van he was driving. We had just bought it about six months ago. He even jokingly called it a "rape van." It was an all-black Ford Econoline with tinted windows all around. We bought it so Charlie could fit all the bikes, kids, and dog inside rather than adding bike racks with locks to my minivan. He wanted to take them all on various adventures and such. His mom kept feeling like there was something there—maybe the guy we bought it from had a warrant out and it was flagged. I was pretty skeptical, and we'd already registered it, but hey, I'd take any explanation at this point.

We got to the jail and walked inside. I was carrying Milo on my hip in a ring sling—he was still too young for preschool and he was also young enough that he thankfully wouldn't understand where we were or what was going on. We asked to see Charlie. The lady at the front told me that you couldn't just visit someone in jail, you had to have made an appointment. And the soonest we'd be able to do that would be tomorrow. *What? Seriously?* Clearly, we didn't know how any of this worked. I knew better than to argue with her, especially when I had a baby strapped to me. Fine, nothing we could do

here. We walked out. That was a total bust.

I called the number the lady gave me from my phone and scheduled to see him tomorrow morning. I gave her my name and birthday as well as Charlie's mom and Milo's info too. We hung up and started to head back to the car. My phone immediately rang. It was the jail. The lady I just made the appointment with told me that due to the nature of the charges, Milo wouldn't be able to come for a visit. *What? Why not?* I was confused again. Milo was his son, why couldn't he come? She repeated that because of the charge, Charlie could not visit with ANY minor. *Well fuck. OK then.* I took his name off the list. Now I also needed a babysitter, which was not something I was super comfortable with. I was not even sure who I could call. I would figure that out later, I guessed.

After I hung up with them, we ran into the bail bondsman. I don't even know how I knew it was him, but I did. He had just come out of the jail after checking on Charlie. I shoved my phone at him. My background was a photo of Charlie with all of the boys.

"Is this him? Is this who you saw?" Part of me hoped it wasn't.

"Yes," he said, "That's him." My heart sank again. Well at least I knew he wasn't dead.

"How is he," I asked? "He's OK—shaken up, but OK." I was so grateful that someone was able to check on him even if it wasn't me. I thanked him and told him that I would be in touch just as soon as we heard about what was going to happen at the bond hearing. I'd already initiated a transfer of money, but I didn't want to close any doors just yet.

We got back in the car and headed to my house. We had a couple hours until we needed to be at the lawyer's office and Milo needed his morning nap. We were both grateful that Charlie was alive but still so confused as to what was actually going on. As I drove, I realized, *shit—I*

have to call his office. He was MIA at work. I didn't want him to lose his job over this. While I knew he'd not been happy there for a while, whatever was going on shouldn't be what decided how that ended. I also then realized I didn't actually know who to call. I didn't even know what his title was anymore. When I had left my job, it also had cut me off from knowing anything about Charlie's position. He would say that things were hard, and he didn't want to mix up the good that was us and the family with how messy it was at work. He literally never spoke about his role or what was going on with the company.

Since I used to work for the same company, I decided to call the contacts I did know. Someone there would know how to get the message to the right people. I tried a few people—some through Facebook and some through old, stored numbers in my phone. I also called the main line and left a message. I hoped that at least someone would get it to whomever he reported to. I used the same story: it was a family emergency, and I didn't expect him to be in all week, but he'd be in touch as soon as he could. He'd been there 12 years and was well respected, so I knew they would take that as sufficient information to explain his absence. I was so grateful; one less obstacle.

We got back to my house and I put Milo down for his nap. I hadn't eaten anything yet and I was running on pure adrenaline. I kept pacing around the house. I needed to DO something, but I didn't know what that something was. Charlie's mom was trying to keep me calm. She kept offering new theories or possibilities that could explain what was happening. I mostly ignored her. *Fuck – I had to call my mom!* She was literally on her way to my house right then. There was no option to keep this from her—she was going to be here tomorrow.

I called her, and she picked up. She and my stepdad, had flown from Hawaii, where they lived and I grew up, to Phoenix and were driving the rest of the way to

Colorado. I told her what had happened. I immediately followed up with saying I had to stick by him and figure out what was going on here. She said of course, of course, but I didn't actually believe her. I could feel the judgment already. I sucked it up and eventually hung up. It was time to wake up Milo and go visit the lawyer.

The lawyer worked out of a small office along Main Avenue in downtown. All the buildings were old and creaky. We figured out which one was his and waited in the lobby for him to be ready to see us.

Eventually we were called in and sat down to try and explain what we knew. Charlie's mom was offering her theories. We both kept repeating that none of this made any sense. This wasn't Charlie. The lawyer listened and said he could help. He would need a $20,000 retainer and then he could call Charlie on the non-recorded lines at the jail and get some more information. *OK cool*—I agreed. I had the cash in the checking account and could write him a check right away. As I started to do that, my phone rang. I picked it up. I had to accept the charges for the call. It was Charlie.

I accepted the charges and answered the phone. He sounded so scared. I very quickly told him I knew where he was and what the charges were. He said this was the first time that they let him call me. He said he'd been trying to get them to let him call me all night. I didn't want him to say anything more, knowing they were recording his calls. I told him I was currently in a lawyer's office and was about to pay him a retainer so he could talk to him confidentially. Charlie was not to say anything else to me. I said, "I love you, and we will get through this." I hung up and finished writing the check.

The lawyer asked us to step out of the room so he could make the call. Charlie was his client, not us. He was very clear about that when I gave him the retainer. We left the office, and I let Milo down to toddle around the

waiting room. I was quiet and nervous. *What could possibly be the explanation here?* I was starting to think there was more going on than I knew, but all of this still made exactly zero sense.

After 10 minutes, the lawyer called me back into his office. Just me this time, not his mom, to which she was pretty taken aback. I left Milo with her and went in. He had notes from his phone call with Charlie. He summarized them for me. There was an online ad that Charlie had responded to. He said he was trying to help them—he thought it wasn't real. *Huh?* I was still so confused. *An ad for what?* My mind was trying to process what he was telling me and it wasn't working very well. The lawyer said the next steps were to get through the bond hearing. We needed to be prepared for Charlie not to be allowed to come home or to see the kids. He was going to try what he could do to get some type of communication allowed, but we should know that might not happen.

OK then—we left his office and headed back to my house. There was really nothing else to do. Charlie's mom was trying to get me to tell her what was said, and I was super close lipped. She asked, "So, it's real?" and I looked at her with pain in my eyes. She got it and dropped the questioning. After we drove back to my house, she headed home and I went to pick up the boys from school.

That afternoon my phone rang, and it was an unknown local number. The caller identified himself as one of the detectives on the case. He wanted me to come in so he could talk to me in person. He said he knew I must have a lot of questions and he would like to help answer them. I saw right through this tactic and told him I was going to have to talk to an attorney before agreeing to meet him and I would call him back later. I also wanted to know where our van was and when I could get

it back. He said he would get back to me about the van, because the authorities were still processing it. *Who did this guy think he was, trying to get me to turn on my husband?*

I fed the boys dinner and tried to calm my mind. I was a total wreck, but I knew I had to try for the boys.

That evening, I called my good friend, Morgan. I knew that I needed someone to help me with Milo in the morning. She was the only one I could think of to leave him with that he already knew. I told her what was going on, and to my surprise I didn't feel judgment from her. She had always liked Charlie and reminded me that he was a good man. There had to be an explanation that made sense. She also agreed not to tell her husband what was happening just yet and came right over in the morning. Her husband Greg and I used to be very close, but over the years that changed, and I became closer to Morgan as we were both stay-at-home mothers. I was terrified of anyone finding out what was going on, and still hoped it was somehow going to just go away.

The next morning Charlie's mom came over again and helped me get the boys off to school. It was a normal school day for them. Morgan arrived to watch Milo, and Charlie's mom and I left to drop off the other two boys just like yesterday, and headed back to the jail.

This time we had an appointment. The lady told us that we would be meeting with Charlie over video. *Wait, what? We couldn't actually see him?* Nope, that's apparently protocol. *Well shit, that sucks.* We only had 30 minutes. She led us to a room with about twenty old school CRT monitors, the big ones that looked to be at least twenty years old. We connected and waited. Charlie came on the screen. He looked exhausted, and was disheveled. He'd clearly been crying and seemed so scared. I shared with him that the lawyer would meet him at the bond hearing. Everyone seemed to think his bond would get reduced so he just needed to hang tight. If it didn't get reduced, I

would still get him out, but I was hoping his bond would get reduced. He agreed with my logic and said he was doing OK. We knew we couldn't ask any real questions about what was happening, but we wanted him to know that we were there for him. We ended the video connection after telling him we would see him that afternoon in court.

As we left the jail, my phone rang. It was a police officer informing me I could pick up my vehicle at the impound lot. I didn't want them to hold onto it any longer than necessary, so we headed right there.

The impound lot was near the hospital in this small, gated building, mostly deserted, with no one even on duty. You had to have someone meet you out there to let you in. The cop was pulling up just as we got there. He handed us the keys, and I signed out the vehicle. In the back I got a look at the van. It had bright yellow EVIDENCE stickers over every door.

Inside they had left a paper roster on the passenger seat of all the things they confiscated as evidence. I was in the driver's seat, and Charlie's mom saw it first. She picked it up and her face fell. "I'm so sorry," she said, as she handed it over. They had taken his work computer, iPad, and phone. They'd also taken condoms he had on him and a bunch of cash. It was more evidence that really did not look good. We never even used condoms, and so I really didn't like what any of that implied. I did not allow myself to slow down long enough to thoroughly question anything. I kept hold of the idea that there had to be a reasonable explanation for everything.

I drove the van to a grocery store parking lot and parked it as far away from the other cars as I could, with Charlie's Mom behind me in my car. It was a difficult vehicle to drive and neither she or I thought we actually could get it backed into the driveway safely. At least this way it was out of police hands. My plan was to get help

moving it again when my step-dad arrived that evening.

We headed back to my house. I was a wreck but doing my darndest to stay calm. Charlie's mom was trying to help. She kept talking to me, trying to reassure me. I needed space. I hid in my room to nurse Milo and just pretended I was fine. Eventually, it was time to head to the courthouse.

Charlie's sister decided she also wanted to show support at the courthouse. We figured it couldn't hurt to have us all there. His sister, myself, and his mom all walked into the courtroom and took our seats. After the judge was seated, they brought in the accused prisoners. Dressed in orange, with shackles on their hands and feet, in walked about 10 men. All of them looked disheveled, and with their heads down. Charlie was among the group of them. I had never seen him looking like this. He looked as if he was trying very hard not to cry. His hair was all over the place, and his pants were so big that they were hardly staying up. He probably hadn't even showered in two days. I smiled at him and he barely peeked up back at me. I saw him try to eek out a smile back, but we could all feel how difficult this was. They cuffed the prisoners hands to the jury bench and started going through the bond cases for the day. There were a few other men present who were accused of the same charge. This appeared to be a fairly large operation. The room was quite busy now. There were federal agents everywhere as well as multiple people from the DA's office.

What we began to understand through the bond hearings was that this was some kind of sting operation that had captured multiple defendants trying to solicit sex from minors. We still didn't grasp most of the details, only that somehow Charlie was caught up in this situation. They called one man who had crossed state lines up from New Mexico and his case was immediately

moved to federal court. Another man with the same charge got his bond reduced like they had predicted. I was hopeful that it meant good news for us. Finally, they called Charlie's name, and his lawyer spoke. Charlie had ties to the community, a family, and he pointed to all of us in the stands. He had a stable job, he was not a flight risk, etc. I was surprised in a way how much it seemed like it did on TV. The lawyer asked for bond reduction down to $100k and permission to have video calls with his kids.

Then the prosecution spoke. He said that in Charlie's particular case, they were anticipating that he would be charged with a more serious crime, from Attempted Human Trafficking to Human Trafficking. The specific facts of his case made them believe they could successfully make a case for the more serious charge, and therefore they were seeking to NOT reduce his bond. They believed he was a danger to his own children as well. There was some commotion in the courthouse, as this was not expected. The judge called both attorneys to the bench so she could hear their arguments. We couldn't hear what was being said. They stepped back and the judge ruled that they were not reducing his bond at this time. That's it. Next case.

I didn't think it was possible to shock me further at that point, but it was. Charlie's head was down and he was visibly sobbing now despite all attempts to keep it in. We watched them take all the men back out and left the courtroom. I didn't have any idea what to think now.

Charlie's mom went to pick up the boys from school and we all headed back to my house. Morgan was there with Milo, now Charlie's mom and sister too. They were all in just as much shock as me and were all trying to talk to me about what to do next. Charlie's mom kept saying to me over and over that Charlie was a lot of things – but he wasn't *this*. I knew that, and I knew he loved his kids.

This was just heartbreaking. I checked the bank accounts. I had initiated two transfers in hopes that I wouldn't need most of it. I was both surprised and relieved that they both went through and there was enough money available now to bail him out.

My phone rang. I had to accept the charges for the call—it was Charlie again. I picked up the phone and told him I was coming to get him anyway. We could talk more when he wasn't on the recorded line. I was packing his stuff so that he could stay at his mom's house. We'd figure out how to get him his car later, but that was the plan for now. I loved him and would see him soon.

Then I called the jail. I could not imagine they wanted me to bring them $250,000 in cash, but I didn't know whom to make the cashier's check out to. They insisted they still wanted cash until I reminded them of the amount. They put me on hold and finally came back with how to pay them via check. I had to move quickly, or the bank would be closed, and I'd have to wait another day.

At the bank I got in line and set up the cashier's check. Next, I went to the jail to get him out. The front office was busy that evening. Multiple people were checking out or bringing money and supplies to their family members. I got the paperwork I needed and started the outtake process. Eventually everything was complete, and I just had to wait.

Charlie came out wearing the same clothes he'd worn when he left for work two days ago. He had the same look as he did in court. He was anxious and a mess. We finished the paperwork and walked out to the car. Once the car doors closed, he instantly broke down in tears. I just watched and gave him some time. I knew I needed to let him get it all out. He wiped his eyes, looked up and said, "Get me the fuck out of here." I started driving.

I drove in the direction of his mom's house. I wanted an explanation, but I also knew he'd been through a whole lot and it might not come right away. About halfway there he started to talk. He said he saw an ad and responded; same as the lawyer had said. He thought it wasn't really real, that it was some kind of scam, but he had to be sure. He told me he was trying to report it to the authorities. He had no idea that it was a sting, and he just wanted them to listen to him so he could explain. He kept repeating over and over that he didn't think it was real. They wouldn't listen to him, wouldn't let him call me. Why wouldn't they let him call me?

I was so confused. *An ad? An ad for what? How long has this been going on?* I still didn't get it. Nothing about this made any sense to me.

He very flippantly responded telling me this had been going on "like, forever." *What has been going on for forever?* I was going to need him to spell this one out.

Then he explained. Seeing escorts. That's something he's been doing since forever. It had been an ad for escorts, and he had started seeing them regularly when he was in his 20s. He just kept acting like this was no big deal. I was quiet. My feelings did not match his reaction, but I wasn't sure what I was supposed to feel.

My husband has been seeing escorts? What??

And on top of that, clearly, he was in a ton of trouble, trouble that didn't seem to match the crime that he was admitting to. I was pretty sure that what he was charged with could put in prison for many years. He started rambling now, asking if I thought he should run. It would mean forfeiting the bond money but maybe the boys and I could join him later. He was so scared and shaken. I dropped him off at his mom's house telling him that this was not something he needed to decide now. Running wasn't the answer. We were going to get through this.

I couldn't head home just yet. My mom had just arrived in town and wanted me to meet her and my stepdad at a restaurant for dinner. I was not capable of hunger at the moment, but still needed help moving the van back to the house, and so I agreed to meet them at the restaurant. As I arrived they were just finishing up. I hugged my mom, and tried to show her that I was OK. I knew she could see right through me, but I also wasn't in any position to break down. I had to stay strong.

They finished up, and we left the restaurant and headed for the grocery store parking lot. My stepdad got in the van and drove it back to the house for me. I wanted him to pull as far into the back driveway as he could. Those big yellow evidence stickers really bothered me and I didn't want to have any nosy neighbors questioning what was happening. My stepdad tried to see if he could remove the stickers, but they seemed near impossible to get off. We'd have to leave it for now.

I had barely seen my kids all day. Milo was anxious to nurse. He wasn't used to time without me. Morgan had tried to get him to sleep but he kept waking up looking for me. I took him and got him to sleep. Then I checked on the other two boys who were worn out from all the attention and people around.

As the evening finally calmed, I found myself sitting in a house full of people wanting the same answers I did. They all wanted me to tell them exactly what happened and how Charlie was not guilty, that this was all a mistake.

But, I could not tell them that. In fact, I could hardly talk to them at all. I didn't want to drag them into this. I had started to come to the realization that this was not going away and that we were maybe even in some danger ourselves. I was the only one with marital privilege that would be protected with any information he told me. I had the thought that any minute the authorities were likely coming to raid the house. It only made sense they

would with what they believed about Charlie. I didn't tell my family anything.

My mind was spinning with the idea that I could potentially lose my kids too, guilty by association or something. What if they found something in the house, and assumed I had to be in on this, whatever exactly this was. I pushed that thought out—I was not going to let that happen.

Eventually it got late, and everyone left—my mom and step dad to their hotel, everyone else to their houses, and it was just me alone with my kiddos. I was still in so much shock, but at least I knew one thing: he was alive and safe for now. What was coming next, I had no clue, but we would deal with it as a family. We could sort out the rest of it all later, once this crisis had passed.

Chapter 2

I was so certain that my husband was a good man. Yes, he was sometimes absent, and we certainly didn't spend time with each other like we used to—that was all true. But at his core, he was a good father and a good husband. Things had never been bad between us. I wouldn't even say they were not good. We literally never fought about anything. That all had to count for something, right?

So many thoughts swirled around in my head. As tired as I was, sleep did not come easily. My mind could not stop all the scenarios running through my mind.

What if the cops showed up while the boys were sleeping? It would make sense that they would come sooner than later. I walked outside around the front porch trying to see if the night air could calm me. As I leaned on the deck railing I saw a cop car drive up the road, turn around at the cul-de-sac and drive back down. My upper middle class, very white neighborhood had no through streets so I knew that this was not just a normal patrol. We pretty much never saw cops in the neighborhood. My heart started racing. I knew they were checking on me. Checking on him. The cop slowed in front of the house, I watched, and he kept going. I finally let out the breath that I didn't know I was holding.

I went inside and grabbed my laptop. I immediately started running a backup of everything on it to cloud storage. If they came into the house I knew all computer devices would be confiscated. Who knows if we'd ever get them back. Baby photos, bills, my whole life was on the computer. I told myself better to be safe than sorry. If they didn't come tonight I'd have a backup completed at least. I thought it might be smart to try and keep my

laptop in the car. I figured they'll have to let us leave if they show up. At least I really hoped that's how it worked. The idea of a team of agents storming the house with my kids watching completely terrified me.

My mind wandered back to my husband. He was a good man, a good father. He loved our boys. I really had to stick this out and see him through it, for the boy's sake if nothing else. Not to mention, how absolutely terrified I was thinking about being solely responsible for three kids.

My own father had been mostly absent in my life since I was nine. He mentally and emotionally abused my mom for most of their marriage. The day he hit her across the face hard enough to need multiple root canals, was the last straw for her. Throughout their court proceedings, he eventually decided to sign over custody. After that we only saw him on birthdays and holidays if we were lucky. As I got older, it sometimes included a rare Friday pizza night.

As a teenager I blamed my mom for his absence. I knew that he had hit her one time, but that didn't seem to justify taking my dad away. I knew he wanted to see us more than we were allowed. I would see him in secret, meeting him at the tennis courts in town after school and never tell her.

When I was 12 I found out my dad's girlfriend lived only a few blocks from us. I was going door-to-door in my neighborhood fundraising for a marching band overnight trip, and as I rang the doorbell, I was completely shocked when my dad answered the door.

In high school sometimes his girlfriend would drive me to school in the morning. Her office was close to my school that was 45 min away in the city, and I really preferred the drive over taking public transportation. So I'd leave my house, with my mom thinking I was walking to the bus stop, only to walk two blocks right over to her

house. She'd usually feed me a bagel or smoothie for breakfast and sometimes I'd even get a packed lunch.

The more time I got to spend with my dad in secret the angrier I got with my mom. My dad would tell me his side of what happened during their divorce. How, yes, it was wrong that he hit her, he agreed about that. He knew that living together wasn't a good idea anymore. They fought all the time and lived in separate parts of the house for most of my childhood. But even when the proceedings started he told me that he had trusted her to do the right thing. She had more resources in the legal system than he did. She was a well known mental health professional in the community. All the litigation was doing was depleting financial resources he didn't have.

He even showed me copies of divorce documents that showed that we were supposed to be with him every other weekend, and every Wednesday for dinner. That had never happened and I didn't understand why not. We did have regular supervised visitation with him for a while when they first split, but that stopped too. He said she had tried to change the time slot and when he didn't agree visitation just got canceled. According to him, everything was her fault.

In the end my dad felt he had no choice but to sign over custody to her. He thought even after everything she'd still let us at least visit him. He would have agreed to anything she wanted, as long as he got to still see us. He was done with the court and done fighting. But he had no idea she was going to take everything. The house, the kids, everything. All he got was the yacht club membership and his van that he was living in. He was very bitter, even many years later.

He even told me he had tried to pay the child support bill multiple times but it kept getting returned to him. He eventually just gave up. He decided to stay off-grid and figured when we were older we'd come find him. Nothing

he owned was in his name. He wasn't even allowed to have a driver's license because he was default on child support. But that didn't stop him from playing tennis with his friends and working under the table cash jobs at the yacht club. All he wanted was to live life to the best of his ability and reconnect with us when we were older and away from her.

I certainly didn't blame my mother for separating from him. I had zero memories of us as a happy family together. But I did blame her for not letting us see more of him. She could have allowed more than she did.

So, for me this meant I was damn determined not to take my kids' father away like my mom had taken mine away. My kids deserved to have their father in their life. I also knew he had a better chance of getting through this with my support, and therefore I felt I had no choice but to support him.

Chapter 3

The next morning was Friday. We had a meeting with the lawyer first thing. My mom was here for another week to help with the boys and Morgan was also planning to come over and help.

When my mom arrived I made sure to tell her that I suspected the cops may show up. Honestly, I was surprised they hadn't already. So, if and when they did, she was not to resist, but get the kids out of the house immediately. I had my computer on me, and she just needed to worry about the boys. I was terrified to leave and not be able to protect them, but I also knew we needed to keep moving. Between my mom, stepdad, and Morgan, I knew they would be safe.

I was also hoping to get some more answers out of Charlie. We hadn't talked more and I still was so confused. What exactly had my husband been up to with these escorts? Now, I wasn't stupid, but I really didn't understand why. We were intimate two-to-three times a week even six years into our marriage. With the exception of when he was traveling, I almost never denied him sex. I mean, for goodness sake, I had basically been pregnant the majority of our married life!

Deeper down, I also knew that he had some desires that I hadn't been willing to fulfill. Early on in our relationship he had asked to have a threesome with me and another man. He wanted to watch me having sex with someone else and then "finish me off." That was a fantasy of his, and it was not something I was comfortable with. He romanticized my teenage wild years, and expected me to be that same promiscuous young girl with him. He would make me feel guilty for doing sexual favors with those meaningless encounters,

and then refusing them with him.

He got so insistent I even considered it for a while, and consulted my closest friend at the time, Greg (the same Greg that was now Morgan's husband) about what to do. Maybe this was something I should do for him? Greg talked me back into my senses, saying no, this was playing with fire. Best case scenario he likes it, but then wants to do more of it, which I really didn't want. Worst case, he hates it and never forgives me. Neither of those worked for me.

Eventually, once we had kids, the pressure to perform sexual acts with others subsided. I assumed he'd gotten over it, realizing that I was more than content with him. Our sex life stayed active and enjoyable. At least I thought it was.

I thought maybe this was what the escorts were about. Or maybe there had been more that he wasn't willing to share with me that he wanted after I had denied the first request.

I picked him up at his mother's house, and we spent a couple of hours at the lawyers office. Criminal proceedings were much more complex than I realized. Nothing would be known for a while. The legal team would have to go through every document, report, evidence, etc from the prosecution before he'd have any kind of idea of what we were looking at. They were just starting to receive everything and it would probably be weeks.

Charlie repeated again and again that he was innocent. He shared that when he first got pulled over he thought it was because he was swerving as he was trying to google how to contact homeland security and report these people offering children for sex. He said there was an email he started to send to report it as well. He was scared to send it, thinking he could get in trouble even for talking to them.

He told the lawyer he was scared to report anything for fear of getting caught. He insisted he only showed up to meet them to determine if it was real or not. If it was real and there were children in danger, he definitely was reporting it. If it wasn't, he didn't want to get in any kind of trouble. He knew something was off, but mostly he thought that they were out to scam people and steal their money. He said the thought of a sting operation never even crossed his mind.

The lawyer told him to send everything all over. He wasn't going to make any promises but he would go over everything.

We left the lawyer's office, and decided to go for a drive. My mom and Morgan were OK with the boys for a while longer and we needed to talk. I believed what he told the lawyer. It made zero sense to me that he would target children. He was the kind of person that always had to solve the puzzle, and understand everything about a situation. I could see where maybe he thought he'd be able to figure this out.

We drove up the valley into the mountains. It was still covered in snow and so we couldn't go as far as we wanted. I parked the car. I was scared. He was scared. What was going to happen? Would he go to jail? Would things get even worse?

The only person I wanted to comfort me throughout all this was Charlie. He was my husband, and my person. And how could anyone else even begin to understand? All the times he was absent, or late coming home—as soon as he walked in the door I would feel better immediately. It always felt like I couldn't stay mad at him once he was in my presence. Everything was just OK again because he was there.

What would happen to him? To us? To the boys? It didn't seem fair. He was being portrayed as a predator, when that wasn't entirely true.

He was beating himself up. He should have seen it coming. He thought he was arrogant enough to solve the puzzle and not get caught. I really didn't know what to say.

I was grateful he was alive, and here with me. And terrified for the future. We kissed. I missed him so much. I missed him before, but this was different. There was a need in both of us. To be connected, to be a part of each other. To reach out to the only person who might be able to help.

We climbed in the back seat of the minivan. The sex was quick, urgent, needy. Neither of us said anything. I'm not sure if we felt better or worse after, but that wasn't the point.

I turned the car around and headed back. Charlie needed to pick up his car from the house, and I had to get back to the boys. Ethan's birthday celebration was tonight. He was six today. Tomorrow was the combined birthday party for Axel and Ethan. Friends and family were all rallying to come over and make tonight special for Ethan. We all hoped he just wouldn't notice that his Daddy wasn't there.

That evening my mom, step-dad, Charlie's mom, Charlie's sister, her husband, Morgan, Greg and their son, all gathered around to celebrate Ethan's sixth birthday. No one said a word about his Dad or what was happening. Ethan gleefully ate cake, and opened his presents.

Once the party subsided, and the kids were put to bed, I again found myself alone in my house. Still scared, but now determined. I was going to protect my children at all costs. I was going to get our family back together. I had no idea what I was going up against. I had no idea what that even meant. But I was going to do it anyway.

The programming in me was so strong to put family first. I was only focused on what was best for my kids and

best for Charlie. Anything that was best for them had to be best for me too.

When big trauma occurs in a person's life, there is always an initial reaction or response. Usually it comes down to fight, flight, or freeze. The body is completely full of adrenaline and those are the only options. My default had always been to fight—fight for my family, fight to protect my kids, fight for our security. So that was exactly what I set out to do.

Chapter 4

Today was Saturday. Another big day. The older boys had a soccer game, and then in the evening was their big birthday party. Because their birthdays were only two years minus six days apart we always did one bigger party with all of their friends together. With everything going on, I had considered canceling, but my mom was here, and I really didn't want to punish the boys for something I couldn't even explain to them.

My friend Morgan met me at the soccer field to help. Today was picture day for the soccer team and we had to be there early. My mom was coming later for the game. I was so stressed and antsy, and I had all kinds of thoughts constantly racing through my head. I tried really hard to be there and present with the boys, but it was not easy.

My mom got there just as the game was starting. Ethan was out with the team playing. Axel was holding back, more timid. Getting him to play had been somewhat of a challenge but we had been making progress. That day, I was OK with him sitting on the sidelines, watching, and feeling everything out.

My step dad started passing the ball back and forth with Axel on the sidelines. He seemed to enjoy that more than what was happening out on the field. My mom watched them for a while, noticing how much fun Axel seemed to be having. She looked over at me and said "You know, I think Axel could really use some more one-on-one time with you."

Fuck. Ouch.

Those words stung me so hard. Here I was sitting with my three children at a soccer game with my husband just out of jail for Attempted Human Trafficking. What fucking extra time did I have? Now, my own

mother is implying I'm not giving my children what they need? Her words hit me deep in my insecure motherly core.

I looked back at her and with a death stare in my eye I said, "Fucking seriously Mom? How dare you!? You're saying that to me NOW?" I was livid. She looked up and realized how I took what she said. I knew how sensitive she was and right this moment I did not care one bit if I hurt her back.

She got up, grabbed her things and walked away. We didn't see her the rest of the game. I only assumed she'd show up at the party later that day.

Morgan saw the whole thing happen. She knew my relationship with my mother was strained. She never quite understood because her own mother was her closest confidant. She looked at me and said, "Wow, I get it now." I shook my head, trying to shake off any guilt I could. How fucking dare she.

After the game I took the boys home for naps. Charlie's family, and Morgan agreed to help me with executing the party. We ordered sub sandwiches, cakes, party favors, and pretended everything was just fine. I really just let everyone else take over the planning and preparations for me. It was so much easier that way.

The party was at the local gymnastics center, a place the boys all knew and loved going to regularly. It was a perfect place for them to play with their friends, and have everyone be occupied with their own children.

I felt immense guilt that Charlie wasn't going to be there to participate. He loved celebrations like this. I knew he was upset that he was missing their birthdays. I tried to ease it by taking tons of pictures and sending them to him as all the party things were happening. I took on a role of photo documenter so that he maybe would feel like he wasn't missing out. It was important that I document everything I could to share it with him.

A few people at the party did ask where he was, but using work as an excuse, no one pushed for more details. There were plenty of adults helping wrangle the children around the gymnastics center. We served food, had cake and opened presents. Eventually everyone left, and we cleaned up. One more obstacle completed.

The following week Charlie had a few additional meetings with the lawyer I hired and although we really didn't know what to look for, he wasn't feeling very confident with his approach either. He wanted someone more sure of an outcome, and with more experience with this kind of charge. Durango wasn't a very big town, so I got the idea that he should ask some other contacts he had if they had a criminal lawyer recommendation. It would mean some disclosure to them, but I figured it would be worth it. He agreed it was worth a shot.

He went over to an ex-coworker's house. She had just started a new company and had corporate lawyer connections. We figured that lawyers would know other lawyers and so she might be able to find someone to help. I really hoped that she would believe his innocence and would want to help us. I also knew that this particular ex-coworker deeply respected his intellect, and thought of Charlie as a good friend.

I was right. She told him that if it had been anyone else she wouldn't have believed them, but they had worked together for so long, she felt she knew how his mind worked so she was going to believe his story. That made me feel so much better. Someone else believed him too. Someone else could see that he wasn't this person the prosecution made him out to be.

After a couple of days she was also able to get a recommendation for a lawyer in Denver that was specifically known and respected for cases like this. Everyone else we spoke to said that to fight a charge like this one, this was the legal team he needed.

He decided to drive up there right away to meet with them. He wasn't allowed to leave the state, but making the six-hour drive to Denver was acceptable. They turned out to be what you might call "sharks" and took a very aggressive stance with lots of experience in these types of sting operations. He felt more confident with them, and so we paid the new $50,000 retainer, and switched legal counsel. At this point I was holding onto hope that we could get this to all magically go away and I was willing to pay whatever it took to get him out of this mess.

He'd been out of jail a week now. I was feeling hopeful. We had support, a new shark lawyer, and a plan.

Charlie had also met with his job and disclosed more of what was happening. The HR department head had been very understanding and compassionate. They agreed to hold his position and keep him out on unpaid administrative leave for now. It bought us some time.

Then the bottom dropped out from under me again. I got a text from Charlie's coworker who helped us find the lawyer. An article had just come out in the paper detailing the case, and naming him publicly.

Fuck. Now the world knows.

The news reporter also seemed to have more details about what happened than I did. My heart began racing a million miles an hour. The walls around my house all of a sudden didn't feel safe anymore. I felt exposed. It was almost as if someone had just painted a giant red A on my door and I had nowhere to hide. The walls were closing in on me. It was not hard to look up where we lived. What if someone decided to take a stance against him? These charges tended to elicit huge emotion in the public. I could no longer keep this from everyone I knew. This was public. I wanted to crawl into a hole with my babies and never get out.

More suspects arrested in child sex sting

Six men face charges for soliciting a minor

By Shane Benjamin Herald deputy editor
Thursday, May 5, 2016 10:07 AM

A child predator sex sting has netted at least three more men suspected of trying to pay for sex with minors in Durango, bringing the total to at least six arrests during a three-day period.

Undercover law enforcement posted provocative advertisements on public websites April 25-27 to lure people in the Four Corners interested in paying for sexual encounters, according to arrest affidavits filed in 6th Judicial Court.

One advertisement, posted on Backpage.com, was titled, "pretty young blossoms ☺ ☺ ☺ —19."

"Hey guys! Krissy here!!! Looking for very open minded no b.s. gentlemen for some fun in Durango!!!! We know how to please!!!! Text for details," the ad reads.

Once callers responded by text message, undercover agents offered to let the men have sex with one or two girls, ages 11 and 14. Agents arranged a time and place to meet, and the men showed up believing they were going to have sex with a minor in exchange for money, according to the affidavits. The men went to different lengths in carrying out the alleged crimes, with some exchanging money and others getting cold feet and driving away.

Those arrested include: Rory Schmier, 47, of La Plata County; Jason Yazzie Chee, 39, of Bloomfield; Harold Marshall, 45, of Farmington; Charles Earhart Watts, 38, of Durango; Christopher Gerard Rindfleisch, 21, residence unknown; and Urunov Timur, 30, residence unknown.[1]

Once that article was out, everyone in town knew. The first call I made the next morning was to the boy's preschool. They knew there had been a family emergency but this was going to shock them.

I got a hold of the director, and she said she would be at school and we could talk then. She had already read the article, and the rest of the staff were aware.

When I got there after checking everyone in, she brought me aside so we could chat. She kept asking,

---

[1] This is an excerpt. To read the full article:
https://www.durangoherald.com/articles/more-suspects-arrested-in-child-sex-sting/

"what happened?" And I just shook my head. All I could give her were facts. We were working through it. I knew her concerns would be for the preschool itself. Other parents would read this and potentially fear for their own children. I assured her he was following every rule the judge laid on him. He wasn't allowed contact with the boys at all, and wouldn't come near the school. She was free to call the police should she see him near campus.

All of a sudden I had a slew of people, friends and acquaintances, reaching out to me to check in and offer to help in some way. Some offered to bring dinner for me and the kids—for which I was grateful. They wanted to do something—and that was something that they could do. But there really wasn't any other way to help. Most of them would drop food off, but also wanted me to tell them more about what was happening with the case. And I really couldn't. I didn't want to jeopardize his defense, and even if that wasn't the issue where would I even start?

I hadn't begun to recover from the state of shock I was in, and there was more fear to be added to it. I walked around the house like a zombie. I took care of feeding and clothing my children, but my mind was always somewhere else.

My mom and Morgan were at the house every day helping me. I was trying to manage the day to day, while also not completely losing my mind. I spent time with Charlie if I could, but mostly I just hid in my head. There was never any conversation between my mom and I about what happened on the soccer field. It just got swept under the rug as usual. Neither one of us was willing to open the can of worms again. It was like this every time we disagreed about anything. She would go somewhere and be in her feelings, and eventually we would pretend it didn't happen.

Her time to head back to Hawaii was coming up. She

asked if I wanted her to stay longer, offering to change her flight. I really didn't want them to stay. I had Morgan and Charlie's family to help me. And, truthfully, I really did not see her as supportive. It was just easier if she left.

The cops also kept driving by my house regularly. Every time they would slow down as they passed by the house, turn around at the cul-de-sac, and drive by slowly again. I was trying not to be paranoid, but it felt like they kept checking in to see if Charlie was here. Which he wasn't—he was at his mom's.

I continued to fear that at any moment they were going to come storming in with a warrant and search the house. I kept my laptop with me just in case, and my nervous system stayed on high alert.

There was a part of me that worried there was actually something to find in the house. Charlie regularly downloaded TV and movies. I was aware that how he was doing it was technically illegal, but I also didn't have any of those login or server details. I knew where the media server was in the garage, but that was the extent of it.

I also just assumed there was porn downloaded too. It was something I knew he watched, but never paid much attention to the specifics. He knew I didn't like watching it myself—to me the girls never looked like they were actually enjoying themselves—and so it wasn't something I really ever found sexy. I also assumed it was something all guys nowadays watched, and so if he didn't insist I participate, who cared?

I eventually just asked Charlie if I should be worried about what they might find. He said he didn't think so but also suggested it wouldn't hurt to take all the hard drives out of his computers and trash them. He said there might be some porn on them, and there definitely were illegally downloaded movies, and so better be safe than sorry. I really didn't want anything to get any worse, so I did as he asked. My heart raced the whole time, terrified I was

actually committing a crime by destroying evidence. I didn't look at what was on those hard drives, I just took them to a Taco Bell drive-through trash can and dumped everything.

The detective on the case continued to try to call and talk to me, he really wanted me to come into the station to discuss the case. I didn't want anything to do with him. I didn't know anything, and I knew that they could only make things worse for Charlie. They were not in the business of "helping" defendants in cases like these.

My family and friends really wanted answers too— answers I didn't have and couldn't give them. Everyone expected me to tell them that it was a mistake and there was a plausible explanation. How could I tell them all that he was actually cheating on me with adult hookers, but that he would never actually try to have sex with children?

Charlie's sister used the analogy that it was like if you were a drug dealer and then all of a sudden some guy offers you a rare tiger. You can't exactly report them, because what you're doing is also illegal. Even if you think what they're doing is much worse, there isn't a way to protect yourself and also report them.

But I couldn't tell my friends or acquaintances that. I really didn't want to tell anyone anything. I feared that if this ended up going to trial any conversations or text messages I had would be considered evidence too.

What I really wanted to do was to run away and never see anyone I knew ever again. I wanted my family safe and away from all this. I wanted to crawl into a safe haven with Charlie and my boys. I would fantasize about finding some deserted island and homeschooling the boys there. We could find somewhere away from all this.

The shock of the arrest, and the change that was being forced in the world around me had me holding onto the truths that I believed to be true with all my

might. We would get through this somehow, that I knew. I had to just keep believing that everything was going to be OK.

As much as I wanted to, I knew that I couldn't actually run away from this. Instead, I just hid as best I could in plain sight hoping to get through this all as unscathed as I possibly could.

Chapter 5

Ten days after Charlie was arrested, he was officially arraigned. There had been a legal review of the case and the sting wasn't as airtight as they thought. The official charge was going to be dropped to Solicitation of a Minor—a much lesser charge. It was still very much a felony but it no longer carried an indeterminate-to-life sentence. It still carried the likelihood of jail time, but not to the extent of what a Human Trafficking charge did. We were confused after what happened at the bond hearing, but also greatly relieved.

I woke up that morning and started to get dressed for court. All the stress I was under meant that I had been struggling to eat anything and was losing a lot of weight. My clothes were getting baggy, which was welcome as I was the largest I had ever been after giving birth to Milo over a year ago. However, there was another problem pulling at me from the back of my mind. My period was late. I tried to attribute it to the stress messing with my cycle, but I knew that wasn't it. I was literally the most fertile person ever, I know how this works. I dug in the back of my bathroom drawers and found some old tests.

Fuck. I was right. The line was faint, but there. I was pregnant. The decision about what to do was made even before I found the test. Abortion was not something I ever thought I would ever even be considering, let alone be capable of making an instant decision about. I would tell myself that I was absolutely pro-choice for others, but it wasn't something I personally could do. But I also never once considered that I would be in the position that I was in either.

From the bathroom, I immediately called Planned Parenthood to make an appointment. I hoped that this

could be done sooner rather than later. I was told that in Colorado, you can't terminate until you're approximately six weeks along because by law they're required to find a detectable heartbeat first. They were able to schedule me for the next available appointment which would be exactly two weeks from then. As much as I wanted it to be over fast, I figured now I would at least have some time to be 100% certain about what I was doing.

I met Charlie at the courthouse for the hearing. We walked in and took our seats, me directly behind him. This time the courtroom was empty and felt very different. He wasn't dressed in orange or shackled amongst the inmates, he was seated on the opposite side of the prosecution in a dress shirt and slacks. His mom and sister weren't there, and there were just a couple of people waiting their turn in the gallery. His new lawyer from Denver was going to be calling in. The hearing was very short—no more than 10 minutes. He was officially charged with Solicitation of a Minor. The restrictions against the children stood. No contact with any minors, period. Bond amount stayed the same. This time it was really just a formality. The next status hearing was scheduled for a month from now.

I had put the older two boys in full time summer camp thinking I was going to have to deal with court hearings more. But, the reality was I was going to have to get used to how slow-paced this actually was going to be.

After we left the courthouse we walked back to our separate cars. I was going to go back home and relieve Morgan, who was watching the boys for me again. I was so grateful for her—she had been at my house every day since this started, helping me with meals and with the boys. I was quiet—trying to think of how to tell him. I knew I had to, but this was too much, after everything. I knew he thought I was simply quiet because of the case. I finally spit it out—I told him I took a test this morning,

and I was pregnant. And quickly added that I'd already made an appointment to terminate. He was surprised— we weren't actively trying to have another baby. But the truth was we never actively tried to have any babies. I was a fertile myrtle and every time there was even a slight possibility, I got pregnant.

He said he understood my decision but was also sad about it. He knew how much I loved my babies. I told him I had no choice but to wait two weeks, so there was time to be certain. Better to have the appointment booked just in case. He reluctantly agreed.

The next couple of weeks were very difficult. Morgan started to be around less, needing to focus on her own family. My mom had gone home. I was now completely alone with just my three children. Charlie's family didn't come around to help as much as I thought they would either. There were still people bringing food over sometimes, but they wanted me to tell them about the case and I really couldn't. Charlie and I were talking on the phone more frequently but that was also getting increasingly difficult.

I started daydreaming what it would be like to have another baby. How I would rearrange the children's bedrooms. This baby would be due in late January, right around Milo's birthday. Maybe even as close as Ethan and Axel's birthdays were. Maybe Milo could have a birthday buddy too. What if this baby was a girl? I'd always wanted a daughter. That thought was particularly challenging for me to stomach. I started spinning in all the possibilities of what another child could bring.

And on the other hand, how could I have another baby now? I had no idea when or if Charlie was going to be around again. I had no idea if he was going to go to prison and if so for how long. Would I have to go back to working full-time? How was I going to support us if I was pregnant or had a newborn?

And then there were the health implications too. My weight was higher than it had ever been. With Milo's pregnancy I had borderline high blood pressure, which could have led to serious complications. I didn't really have a support system either if I was put on bed rest. I was on my own with three young kids who already depended on me 100%.

It was Charlie who finally suggested that I talk to a professional about this decision. I had started to be so torn and unsure of what I initially felt completely confident in. I did a google search of local therapists, and found one who was available to see me right before my appointment. Her website said she specialized in complex family issues, which sounded exactly like what I had going on. I briefed her the best I could before the appointment as I would only get to talk to her once before.

In the session she listened very openly. She heard my situation and my what-ifs. What if the case is dropped and we get to go back to normal? What about when he's back home again? What if it's my girl? She was the perfect sounding board and a voice of reason. As I shared my story of what was happening in my reality and in my head and my heart I could feel myself questioning everything. I was really waffling here. I wanted a way to pretend that everything was going to be OK. I wanted to believe that this was all going to go away soon and our family could be whole again. I had started to see this pregnancy as a way to do that.

In the end, her advice was really simple: write out a pro/con list and put everything on paper—the feelings and the realities. The decision would be made clear to me.

I got home and did exactly as she suggested and wrote it all out. On one column was the pro. I loved babies and I was generally healthy. In the cons I had

things like having borderline high blood pressure during my last pregnancy, and almost wasn't able to have my home birth. This pregnancy would be immensely more stressful than the previous ones. I was responsible for three kids full-time. My own mental health. What if something happened to me? Without anything to say otherwise I had to assume Charlie wouldn't actually be home by then. I'd be taking care of a newborn alone with the other three.

The decision was obvious just like she said it would be. As hard as it was, I really could not have this baby now. It was too much on my body and my health, not to mention the danger to my existing children if something did go wrong. I had to look at this as if I was their only parent. I had to take care of my health first, so that I could take care of them. My intuition was right off the bat. This really was not something we could do right now. I finally felt clear again about my choice.

The abortion appointment was just a couple days later. Charlie was able to come with me while Morgan watched the boys for me. They tell you you'll be at the clinic most of the morning and I had no idea what to expect.

I wasn't feeling particularly nervous about the appointment itself as I knew that everyone in the clinic would be there for the same reason. They schedule abortions only on Fridays, and warn you that as you drive up, there are always a handful of anti-abortion protesters outside.

I ignored the protestors, and went inside. I checked in and started filling out the paperwork. Most of it was pretty standard, although as I got to the part about sexual history, I froze. I knew mine, but the man sitting next to me, the one I shared three children and so much intimacy with, that was another story.

Deep breath, I just moved on, and focused on the

problem at hand. Eventually my name was called to go inside. They explained to me my options, surgical or medical. I choose a medical termination—pills you take to stop the growth of the fetus. It was simple, easy, and in early pregnancy was very effective.

They set me up for the ultrasound, and gave me a choice to see the fetus on the screen or not. I choose to not. I was just ready to get this over with. The staff were all very calm and welcoming and understanding. They talked to me alone to make sure that it was truly my decision and not one I was coerced into.

The week before, I had insisted Charlie get tested for STDs to make sure he wasn't further putting us at risk. Now that I was here already, they tested me too and said they would call if anything came up.

After the ultrasound I was sent back into the waiting room to sit and wait. Eventually it was my turn again, and they handed me the first set of pills to take in the office. I was also given a second set to go home with that would begin the contractions and actually facilitate the expulsion of tissue. They suggested waiting till I was actually able to rest and not having to be active in case the bleeding got really heavy or painful.

As soon as I got home, I started to miscarry. They told me it wasn't supposed to happen that fast. I wasn't going to be taking the second set of pills until the evening after the kids went to bed. But, my body was ready. It was time to let go.

After a few days of laying low, I was back to normal. I healed very quickly. It felt like more of a heavy period than anything. I was grateful that it was over.

I also decided it was time to put myself back on birth control pills. No more chances of that happening again. While Charlie was still not allowed at the house, I still very much wanted to figure out how to heal my relationship with him but I knew better than to leave it to

chance again.

Everything I was doing was to figure out how to make it through this whole ordeal together and as a family. If I could just focus on that, I would be OK.

Chapter 6

After the abortion was over, I began to isolate myself even further. I felt so ashamed. I was ashamed of my husband. I was ashamed of myself. I was ashamed of what my life had become. I didn't want anyone to see any part of what was going on with me either. I completely deleted all social media accounts. The idea of being tagged or messaged about the criminal case overwhelmed me.

Charlie had moved from his mom's house to his sister's house. She was a nurse and both she and her husband worked and traveled a lot and were rarely home. He liked having more time to himself and had more space there than he did at his mom's. It was slightly further out of town, but all he had at this point was time.

She asked Charlie if there was a chance I wanted a treadmill. She had bought one used, and as most people do who have ideals of working out in their homes, she never did. She was clearing out her spare room and didn't want it taking up space anymore. She thought maybe I might like it.

I absolutely did! I hadn't been able to do any kind of exercise for a long time. Three young kids on your own doesn't make it easy. Not that I had done so when Charlie was around either, but now I had more time, just no childcare. I'd been struggling to lose the baby weight, and although the stress of the court case meant I was losing weight rapidly, I also knew I had to take better care of my health.

Charlie and his sister brought it over and set it up for me when the boys and I were out of the house. They put it downstairs in front of the big TV, which was perfect for me to use after the boys went to bed or were napping.

And with that, I started running every day. Well, truthfully it was more like run/walking at first, but I got on the treadmill at some point every day. It was literally just one thing I could do for me. After the boys went down to bed, I would often run/walk three miles. I could finish in the length of a TV show, and doing so allowed me the space to finally turn off my brain.

The more children I had, the more it became difficult for me to put my own needs over anyone else's. There was always someone who needed to be nursed, changed, fed, or played with. Some parts of the house always needed cleaning, and dinner needed to be prepared or made. It was a never ending rotation of responsibility. My own well-being was the last thing on my to-do list. The idea of going to a gym or taking an exercise class, unless I could take all three boys with me, just seemed impossible. Of course there were places with childcare or preschool options, but none of them ever appealed to me.

That treadmill was truly a godsend for my mental health. There was finally a way to move my body without compromising taking care of my children.

One evening just before I was about to get on the treadmill I got a message from Morgan's husband, Greg. It had been years since he had reached out to me directly like this. He knew what was going on through Morgan but he wanted to come over and talk to me personally. He said he had something to tell me.

I told him sure, the boys were in bed and I was just about to go for a run but he was welcome to come by. I got on the treadmill anyway figuring he'd be at least 20 minutes.

Once he arrived he sat on the couch and waited. I got off, and he made small talk for a bit, asking how the running was going, and how were the boys. He wanted to know how I was doing, and to see what, if anything, I

could tell him about the case. I really couldn't share more than what was public, which I explained to him.

He wanted to know about the sting operation. Whether Charlie wanted the 11 or 14-year-old—this seemed important to him. He seemed to be grappling with something, and I very quietly responded, "Both, he asked for both."

"Oh, wow," Greg said. He explained he had been hoping it was just the 14-year-old. In his mind, he explained, a 14-year-old was post-pubescent and, although it was very, very wrong, some part of him at least understood the attraction. An 11-year-old was pre-pubescent and very much a child. I really had nothing to say. I did not like this conversation. I tried to explain Charlie's version and said I believed him—that's not what this was about. I wasn't sure he believed me.

He then said he had something he needed to tell me. A rumor that he'd heard. There had been talk about Charlie sleeping around at the office, and it was seemingly common knowledge enough that it got back to him. Greg hadn't worked at the same company in years, and although at one point we all worked in the same department together—that seemed like a lifetime ago.

I wanted more information. Who told him this? Who was Charlie supposedly sleeping with? I told Greg he had admitted to prostitutes, but Greg was not convinced that's all it was. He believed there was another relationship going on ON TOP of the hookers, and felt it was time I knew. Greg wouldn't give me any details. He refused to tell me how he came to know this, and only shared that he trusted the source.

I didn't want to believe him. This couldn't be possible. Why would he admit to sleeping with prostitutes and not this?

Greg then reminded me that when Charlie and I first got together, he was actually cheating on his second wife,

with ME. In fact we dated in secret for over a year before anyone ever found out. He had convinced 18-year-old me that his marriage was beyond repair and that his wife and he were already in the process of separating.

However, it wasn't until over a year later, that his second wife eventually did move out of their apartment. After that, at my insistence, we came out as a couple and started to be seen together in public. Charlie had been very ashamed that he had been cheating on his wife then, and had wanted to move slowly, but I pushed things out into the open faster. I had been waiting over a year, and was more than ready to be out together.

Before that, he would only ever come over in the middle of the night for a couple of hours and leave before the sun came up.

The realization then hit me. In his second marriage, I was actually the prostitute. No, he didn't pay me for my time, but he certainly treated me as an escape from his other life.

I had convinced myself that somehow I was special. It was true love with us, and that justified his cheating before. I had stuck it out, waiting for him for over a year. Through all the nights he didn't respond to my texts, or the awkward social get-togethers where I had to pretend we weren't sleeping together. I had this belief that because I stuck it out, I had been somehow right about us being meant for each other all along. We moved in together, purchasing our first townhouse, and only a year later I was pregnant with Ethan. We got married, and lived comfortably. We were happy.

There was no comparison to our life and the life he described living with his ex-wife. I did not understand why he would need to escape from me. But he already admitted that he did. So what was the difference?

I was not a happy camper. Somehow I'd convinced myself that meaningless sex was OK, and eventually

repairable, but this would not be.

The conversation then flipped to Greg's own marriage and his struggles as I tried to comprehend what he was telling me and what it meant. For me, it was much easier to focus on the person in front of me than look at my own feelings as I knew he was also going through marital problems of his own.

The next thing I knew he was standing up yelling at me to mind my own business and that I was not to talk to him about "MY WIFE!" He was very possessive and angry with me for bringing it up. Another couple of "FUCK YOUs" and he walked out the door.

What on earth was that about? I had no clue what to think now. I messaged Morgan confused as to what was going on. A part of me was scared to have him go back home to her like that. She apologized for his behavior and said he has been working through a lot of his own mental health problems recently. He came home perfectly normal and so to her this was just another example of his outbursts that she had been struggling with. Greg had really felt I needed to know, but also was not in a good place himself.

Not knowing what to think now, I told Charlie what happened. He denied everything. He said that made no sense to him, and clearly Greg was not doing well so I should just ignore it. He loved me and only me, and there never was anyone else.

And so for now, that's all I knew to do. It's not like any rumor was going to change things anyway.

We were now coming up on a month since the arrest. The boys continued asking where their daddy was. When was he coming home?

Ethan was in the shower one evening and he said, "Mommy, when is Daddy coming home? He's been in Cincinnati a long time."

His question took me by surprise. I didn't even

realize they would just assume he was traveling as he so often did. Usually he was gone for five days at a time, and home most weekends. He'd never been gone this long before.

Not sure what to say, I just responded, "I'm not sure." He wanted to know why not and where he was, and so I told him I would try to think of a way to explain to him what was going on that he could understand.

I knew I had to tell them something and so that night at bedtime I tried to come up with the best explanation I could with what I knew.

I told Ethan that you know how sometimes he gets in trouble for something that he didn't actually do? Whether it was one of his brothers or just a misunderstanding, sometimes even a grown up gets it wrong. Being a very bright kid, with a very literal way of viewing the world, he absolutely did.

I told him that it was kind of like that with Daddy. "The police think that he did something really bad and wanted to hurt people, but he was actually just trying to help them. He's in a lot of trouble for it, but that's not really what happened. And so for now Daddy has to stay away until we can get it all sorted out."

I told him Daddy loved them and missed them a lot, and he hoped he could find a way they could see him very soon.

He seemed to process what I was saying and understand why Daddy was away for now.

I continued my days as best I could with my children. We spent hours at the park, museums, and the recreation center doing the things we always did that they loved. It was summer in Colorado and being outside in the sunshine more was good for everyone.

The boys weren't even allowed to talk to Charlie on the phone. If he called when they were in the car with me, I couldn't answer on the car's bluetooth. I had to be

very careful they were not interacting with him in any way.

One time when I was putting Axel down for his nap, I answered a call from Charlie on my bluetooth headset. He could tell I was talking to Daddy, and wanted to say hi. It broke my heart to continue to tell him no.

At school they started telling their teachers they were sad. They missed their daddy and wanted to see him. All I could say was that he missed them too and would be home as soon as he could.

I knew I had to do something more to help them. I thought that perhaps we could get some type of visitation put in place for them. Charlie's new lawyers thought that with my support it would work. They advised me to get my own attorney so as to not be seen as being working with them and submit a letter on his behalf. They had a recommendation for a lawyer that they had worked closely with before. We set up a call.

There wasn't much to it, as it was really for optics to the court, but my lawyer was able to help me craft the letter for what I wanted. We had to be very careful with our wording, so that they could tell we were taking his charge seriously.

The lawyers were right. With me showing up and supporting him, at the next status hearing, we were awarded the ability to have supervised visitation. My support was incredibly powerful to the court. The children had gone now six weeks without a phone call or a visit, and they could finally see their daddy again!

The very first visit I was nervous that Milo, who was very shy of strangers, might not recognize him. We scheduled it for right after nap time so they wouldn't be overtired, and could play as long as possible. Thankfully Milo did recognize him right away and all three boys were ecstatic that they got to see him again.

Supervised visits were a very welcome change in the

schedule. The boys looked forward to seeing their Dad for a couple of hours one or two times a week. It was like a big Daddy playdate. They got more attention from him than they ever had, and they loved it. We tried to schedule as many of them as we could. They weren't cheap at $60 per hour, but it felt like a very worthwhile expense.

When one evaluator couldn't accommodate the amount of visits we wanted, we found two more to work with as well. It seemed incredibly important to keep their connection open to him and this was, for now at least, the way to do that. One of them commented to me what an amazing father he was to them, and how present he was.

And it was true. He recognized how valuable the time with them was, and made the most of every minute. This was the family experience I always wanted to have and never did. Charlie, present at home with me and the boys. I would be lying if I said I wasn't enjoying myself as well.

That summer our entire schedule revolved around those visits. I'd take the boys out of summer camp if there was a visit scheduled that day. The house would get cleaned, a nice meal would get prepped or made, and we'd spend all our attention preparing everything for those precious couple of hours.

Charlie often would bring over a present or activity we could all play with together. It was warm out and we spent a lot of time out in the backyard or playing board games inside.

After a couple of months of this, it started to get much more difficult for everyone to say goodbye after the two hours were up. The fun was wearing off now that it had been going on so long. Axel especially didn't understand why Daddy had to leave and couldn't stay at home with us anymore. There would be lots of tears and sadness. How to explain to a four-year-old why Daddy

wasn't able to live with us anymore was impossible. I didn't want to stop the visits, but I truly didn't know how much longer we could all keep this up. It was exhausting on so many levels.

For my sanity, I continued running on the treadmill every day. No matter if it was a visit day or not I always made sure to get some exercise in. My weight started dropping really fast. I started losing over one pound a day and I loved it. Weight was literally falling off of me. I was enjoying feeling good in my body again and even dug out all the pre-baby clothes I had been holding onto. I felt sexy in a way I hadn't felt in years.

I found myself flirting with Charlie again, sending pictures of me in new clothes that felt good. I had no one else to share with and I was excited about my body and how I began feeling in my skin. He responded with sexy messages that made me feel good and appreciated. It had been so long since I felt sexy in my body, and I was excited. I had opened a bigger doorway to connect with him in a way that we hadn't since we began dating.

Charlie tried to help me as much as he could with the housework and other chores but it was difficult as he could not be at the house if we were home. I'd go run errands and he'd pop in to clean bathrooms or mow the grass. We'd often have to wait at the corner of the street before we could pull into the driveway if he wasn't done by the time we were. Just sitting in the car, waiting with three kids to go into our house, because the law had deemed my husband unsafe for his own children.

If I wanted to spend any time with him, I would have to find a babysitter who could watch them. And because of the very public criminal case I also had to disclose to them the situation. One girl was absolutely terrified and blocked me after I told her, even though she would never even meet Charlie. After working through recommendations from friends, I did eventually find someone to

watch them for a few hours so we could spend some alone time together.

My emotions skyrocketed from one side of the pendulum to the other. One day I was feeling sexy and flirty and the next I was angry and upset.

One evening as I was running and simultaneously on the phone with Charlie, the anger started to bubble up. I started to cry and wanted to yell and scream. I hung up on him abruptly and started to run faster and faster just wanting to numb the pain. My husband of six years had cheated on me with all those women. He had been faithful for less than a year of our marriage. He had done so while I was pregnant and breastfeeding our three children. He put not only my health at risk—but their health as well. And he did it unapologetically. Tears started to stream out.

My phone was blowing up. He was sorry. He loved me. He didn't deserve me, but he wanted me. Could I see that he has changed now, and forgive him? He immediately drove to the house and left a love note and flowers in the mailbox. He waited outside until I answered so he could check on me.

He would not allow me to feel what was coming up. He made me feel so wrong for having those feelings, because he was clearly trying to show me that time was over, and things were going to be different.

Just like I had done every time he was late coming home or didn't answer his phone, once the tears subsided I let the anger go and told myself it didn't matter. He was here now, he wanted to be with us now. The anger wasn't worth it—it didn't solve anything. It didn't keep the family together. It didn't keep a father in the boys' lives. I truly hoped that he was working on himself. I hoped that this would be the wakeup call that he needed.

His lawyers had him enroll in biweekly therapy. They had a relationship with a particular therapist in Denver,

and strongly recommended that Charlie see him. Since he wasn't working anymore, it was pretty easy for him to drive up every other week and drive back. It kept him busy which he really needed. His mental health was struggling even more than it had before. He had been put on SSRI antidepressant medication and while they helped, they certainly didn't fix anything.

When Charlie wasn't in Denver, he was either mountain biking or visiting us with a supervisor. Once the cops stopped driving by the house, we figured out he could spend evenings at the house, after the kids went to bed, either on the front steps or hiding in the garage so he wasn't having unsupervised contact with the boys. We flipped the door lock around so it could lock from the outside ensuring an unsuspecting child didn't barge in.

He began a project of sorting through old things, going through the mass amount of stuff every household seems to collect over the years.

Once the boys were asleep I would sneak down and spend time with him. As difficult as the case was, there was a part of me that felt like I also was finally getting the relationship I always wanted with him. I had spent years wanting a deeper connection and feeling ignored, and now here he was showering me with as much time and affection as he possibly could.

If we weren't physically together we were on the phone. It got to the point where we were on the phone sometimes literally 24/7. He was in my ear constantly. Every thought I had, he was right there. We told ourselves it was helping us to stay connected.

The duality of the darkness of the case, and the deepening of a connection that I always wanted was not lost on me. Why did things have to be this bad, for them to swing over and be this good at the same time?

Ethan was going into first grade that year and I had enrolled him in a private Montessori program. Ethan is

one of those kids that just doesn't fit the normal mold at all. He had taught himself how to read at three years old, and was already doing multiplication by the time he left kindergarten. At the same time, he was socially awkward and likely was on the autism spectrum, although we never formally tested him. We knew it was important to find a program that would work with him while also understanding some of his quirkiness.

The orientation for the school came and I knew I had to have the conversation with the school about Charlie. This was not going to be a fun conversation but I was the only one to do it. I had to inform his teachers and principal that Ethan's dad was out on bond for attempted solicitation of a minor, and that he had bond restrictions and so he would not be coming to the school, but would want to participate in any parent meetings remotely.

Every time those words left my mouth, I had to deal with the shock on the other person's face. People didn't know whether to be appalled or to comfort me. They wanted to know more, and also didn't. It was incredibly triggering as it required me to relive the experience over and over.

Ethan's new school principal even asked me for a photo of Charlie so that she could pass it around in case he ever came to the campus to take Ethan. Her logic was if things went poorly he might try to come take Ethan and run. I couldn't believe people would think this of my husband.

I knew that this was going to keep coming up. I was going to have to get used to telling other people what happened. I just hoped it would eventually get easier. But for the time being unless disclosure was absolutely required, I did not want anyone else to know the truth of what was going on.

Chapter 7

My little sister was getting married that September. She is my only sibling, and although we weren't very close, she was still very important to me and I wanted to make sure I showed up for her. I was her maid of honor, and so we really had to go. The boys and I flew to Portland. All four of us didn't fit in her house, so I rented an Airbnb close by for just us. I also only wanted to stay the minimum amount of time required to be there for the wedding. I was in such a rush to get back to visit with Charlie, and the kids had just started the new school year, we only stayed three days.

While in Portland, unless I was at my sister's house, I was on the phone with Charlie. Getting ready for the wedding, putting the kids down for a nap—Charlie was on the phone with me the whole time. I didn't go to my sister's bachelorette party—using the boys as the excuse. Really, I felt so disconnected from her and I didn't know what to do about that. I also didn't know what would actually come out of my mouth if given the opportunity and a couple of alcoholic beverages.

Their wedding was in this beautiful outdoor space in central Oregon. It was so green and open. We drove separately since I had three kids in carseats, coming from my Airbnb, and also still had to consider Milo's nap time. There was no service in the area either, so we disconnected from Charlie to be present at the wedding. We arrived and most of the wedding party was already there. We were supposed to be taking photos with the wedding party before the ceremony. There was a beautiful lake in the background, and so much lush greenery.

My mom and sister were the only ones who knew anything about my situation back home. I was really nervous people were going to ask why my husband didn't join us for the wedding. I didn't really know what to say— usually a whole family comes to the sibling's wedding. I wanted to avoid the questions. I'm really not an effective liar. My face always gives any attempt away. And I had enough disclosures recently. I really didn't want to bring any of that to my sister's day.

My focus was just keeping the kids entertained and happy so my sister could enjoy her wedding. The boys had all been so clingy to me, especially Milo. Milo also didn't much like strangers, and I didn't even think he'd let his grandma hold him during the ceremony without screaming bloody murder. My plan was to wrap him on my back in a baby carrier and hope that it helped him to stay calm.

Well, that worked for the first half of the vows. The second half he started fussing. I unwrapped him and handed him to grandma. He immediately started wailing and she took him away so that the rest of the guests wouldn't be disturbed.

Kids are so sensitive, you know—they can feel everything going on around them. They just don't have words for it. They don't know why their tummy hurts or they feel weird. Milo was so connected to my emotions and my stress and would not leave my side for anything. He was like my little miniature energetic protector. It certainly made for a hard time if I needed to leave him, but that has always been part of our connection.

When Milo was a tiny baby, he slept next to me every night. All my kiddos were breastfed/co-sleeping babies. I was not a mom who was interested in getting up multiple times a night to go to their room, nurse them, and try to magically transfer them back down. I tried briefly with Ethan and quickly gave up on that idea. As soon as Ethan

started sleeping with me consistently everyone started sleeping better. More sleep for everyone was definitely my preference.

With Milo, long before he had any words, when he would stir, I would immediately wake up and nurse him back down just like I did with his brothers, sometimes not even hardly waking myself. However, for him—if he woke up and I was not directly facing him so he could see my face, he would scream bloody murder like I had died. Even if it was just my back to him, he wailed and wailed. I started having to move him with me if I needed to change the shoulder I slept on. He did not approve of anything else. That's how important that connection was to him. Knowing that he felt everything I did, only strengthened my resolve to stay strong.

As the maid of honor in the wedding I was expected to give a speech. I had prepared it on the airplane and I felt really good about speaking. I really wanted to say something that would save her from the pain that I was currently living through. My speech felt powerful as I spoke from the heart. I knew my message was received.

"My little baby sister. I was only three when I missed your birth because you were so darn eager to be in this world. I knew then that no matter what, we would always have each other.

When you were two I had to start interpreting for you when you wanted some juice because you just refused to start talking. You were happy as could be in your walker just eating bread crusts and babbling to yourself. I think you knew your big sister would make sure you got what you needed.

You were in elementary school when I taught you how to lie. I would pick you up after school and we would watch our shows before mom came home and then do all of our chores real fast before she would know what we were up to. Whoops, I'm not sure you ever fessed up to that one.

I know I got caught up in my own life once I hit my teenage

years. And then between two marriages and three kids, well... life just gets away from you. When you started dating I really tried to warn you to take it slow, but you just wouldn't listen. Look where that's gotten you.

I'm really so thrilled for the both of you. And so excited for the hopefully soon to be coming cousins. Sorry Bearach (their dog), you don't count.

A couple of pieces of advice from someone who has been through it. Never lose the bubble. You know what I mean. The you and him against the world. The idea that together nothing will stop you. Never ever stop talking and sharing. No matter how bad it is, you've chosen each other to be the ones to go through it with. You have to trust that no matter what, you can and will get through it together.

I love you. I wish you all the best and I know that as long as you do it together it will be amazing."

We left Portland the next day, and headed back to Colorado and all the legal proceedings.

Chapter 8

An additional part of the legal process was having Charlie evaluated as a candidate for probation. We were hoping that a good evaluation would mean he would have little to no jail time. His legal team again chose a very specific evaluator in Pueblo, Colorado, one they were familiar with. They felt that she was the most likely to give him a recommendation that would be positive.

The evaluation was done over an entire day. Multiple interviews, questionnaires, and testing using a video screen to flash images at him to see what he was sexually attracted to. The therapist would interview me, his family, his therapist, and his psychiatrist. It was expected to be very comprehensive.

He spent a day with her, and then a few weeks later she called me for my interview. She told me she felt he was deeply depressed. He could barely look at her during the entire interview. I knew he was struggling, but I didn't know it was that bad. I told her my concern was my children, and having their father in their lives. She told me she had no concerns about him around them—her concerns were more about his mental health than anything.

Her report came back and the lawyers were very pleased. They felt with it that he would get offered a plea deal with little to no jail time, and probation would follow quickly. I asked to read the report, wanting to see if maybe it held another layer of understanding for me.

It was not an easy report to read. Reliving the details of my husband's escapades in detail from a clinical angle was difficult to say the least. And then came another surprise. There was more. Not only had he been with 50+ prostitutes during our marriage, but some of those

included men. Now let me be clear, it wasn't that I cared that he was attracted to men or not. But what I did care about was that after all of this, there were still more secrets and lies. *What else didn't I know?*

And then there was the part I couldn't even admit to myself. On some level I had been comforted by the fact that we had young boys, not girls. My assumption had been that he was only attracted to females, as that had been true to my knowledge. But with this new information, it seemed that was actually irrelevant.

I sat with that report and just breathed. Technically this should be no big deal. The lawyers were happy. This was a good report, they said. The report did say he was primarily attracted to post-pubescent women. Why did it not feel like that? I shoved all my feelings down. I supported him this far—surely I couldn't stop now. A plea deal should be considered a good thing, but I was also faced with the fact that it would come with sex offender registration. It would mean this would never really be over. That stamp would continue to follow us around.

I told him that I wasn't sure I could keep doing this for 10+ years. It was one thing when it felt like there was an end in sight, or even better, the charges being totally dropped. But now that seemed impossible. How was I supposed to be OK with a guilty plea? Everyone would always think on some level he must have been guilty. We couldn't hide in our house forever.

I really didn't understand if he was really innocent. Why couldn't we fight the charge? He told me that he tried to ask the lawyers this, but they believed that if he tried he would most certainly lose. They even did a mock trial to show him how ridiculous the idea would be. There was no proof of his story, and everything the prosecution had was concrete. That did not make me feel any better.

He was actually innocent though, right? Could I really

continue to stick by him that long knowing what I know now?

In my mind, it came back to the same thing. I had no choice but to stick by him for the boys. And he was facing his demons, demons I now knew about. I kept holding faith that this would only make us stronger in the end.

So, my support for him continued. We continued to ask for more time. Eventually, with excellent supervisor reports, I was awarded the supervisor role, so we didn't have to pay for visits anymore. This also meant that Charlie essentially moved back in. He was allowed to be around if I was home too—so since I wasn't working that meant he was always there.

We were all so relieved to have him back in the house full-time. The boys were thrilled he could spend the night again, and I felt so much gratitude to not have to manage the visits and everything that came with that anymore.

And then the final step was support of him gaining unsupervised access to the boys. In Colorado there had just been a change in precedent at the supreme court level. The court deemed that being a sex offender didn't automatically remove your right to parent—as it had previously. This was described below by the Colorado Sex Offender Management Board.[2]

"United States vs. Burns, 775 F.3d 1221 (10th Cir. 2014) impacts Colorado's current approach to parent-child contact and therefore necessitates Colorado re-evaluate its approach. In Burns, the Court ruled that a parent has a constitutional right to familial association. In part, 'A father has a fundamental liberty interest in maintaining his familial relationship with his [child].' Burns at 1223, citing United States v. Edgin, 92 F.3d 1044, 1049 (10th Cir. 1996). The Court continued, stating that

---

[2]https://cdpsdocs.state.co.us/somb/resources/BurnsNarrative-BoardApproved03-18-16.pdf

'When a court imposes a special condition that limits a fundamental right or liberty interest, the court must justify the condition with compelling circumstances.' Id. At 1223. A conviction, alone, may not meet the criteria for compelling evidence for restraining a parent's constitutional right to parental association."

We had to apply for that exception because the official sex offender standards had not yet been updated, but if I stood up in court stating my consent, I knew it would work. That was it. Once it all went through, he would have unrestricted access to the children.

January 4, 2017 was the day he pled guilty to Attempted Solicitation of a Minor. It was also the day he gained back his parenting rights. The DA had done better than the lawyers expected and offered a plea agreement with a lesser felony and no jail time. All he had to do was agree to four years of probation, and complete a sex offender treatment program. He would also be required to register as a sex offender for a minimum of 10 years post completion of his probation. He really couldn't say no to a deal like that.

That was it, the criminal case was over, and we were free again to pick up the pieces of our lives.

Chapter 9

Once we made it through the criminal case and Charlie was back home with unrestricted access to the boys, it was time to tackle the next obstacle. He had been out of work now for over six months and I had been out of work for six years. Thankfully, we still had savings, but it wasn't the kind of money that was going to last forever.

Prior to the arrest, Charlie had received an offer to join a new company doing similar work, and so I pushed him to contact them again to see if he could start work there now. The company had been founded by the same ex-coworker that helped him find his lawyer and so I was hopeful that she was going to be excited to hire him.

He contacted her and started the conversations. She knew his technical skill set was a fit, but she wasn't sure how her investor was going to feel about hiring someone with his offense history.

After some back and forth with her investor, she agreed he could work only as a contract employee. The investor wasn't comfortable hiring a sex offender full-time, but since he didn't control who she contracted to, she decided to try to hire him for contract work anyway. And bonus, by doing that, he could work remotely. It seemed like it was going to be the perfect opportunity to get us back on our feet.

He went into the office, met with the team, and identified what his responsibilities were going to be for the upcoming project that they were working on. They needed support in preparation for their first big audit. He had lots of experience with this type of audit and he knew there were strict protocols and deadlines. He got set up right away. He bought a new work laptop and set up his workstation in the living room.

I was hopeful that going back to a version of normal was going to really help him and me take the next step to start to repair the marriage and our family. It would give us some sense of normalcy to start with.

I continued to take care of the kiddos, getting them back and forth to school and to their various activities. Having Charlie around more meant I didn't have to tout Milo around for every errand which was also a really nice change. I was able to get a run in while the kids were in school without having to worry about waking Milo up, because Charlie could help him, too. He seemed eager to make up for all the time away and be as present as he possibly could.

He'd clean the house with Milo in the mornings so I could run after I dropped everyone off at school instead of having to wait after they went to bed. He cooked breakfast and let me sleep in. He went above and beyond in a way he never had before.

However, I also started to notice that he wasn't getting any work done—he seemed to get distracted constantly. I was pretty certain that after a month went by, he hadn't accomplished a single task. I knew that the company was counting on him for this deadline and that he was in serious danger of leaving them in a bad place. I brought it up with him as delicately as I could —and he admitted that I was right. He broke down. He couldn't focus, and he felt again like he was a complete fraud and failure. The antidepressants that he'd been prescribed during the criminal proceedings just weren't helping enough.

We decided that as much as he wanted to, he was really not in a position to be working yet. I crafted and sent over an email telling the company that he was not in a good place to resume work. We knew that this left them in serious danger of failing the audit, but it was better to tell them now than have everyone think everything was all hunky dory when it wasn't. He left that contract

without having completed a single billable hour.

So, now what? I had already started feeling like it was going to be time for me to go back to work. It had been six years, but I knew the longer I waited the bigger that employment gap was going to get. I refreshed my resume and started sending it out. I signed up for some free online courses to refresh my technical skill set. I also had been in the information technology field, but everything changed so quickly—I didn't want to feel like everything I knew was outdated.

Pretty quickly, I found a job posting by a local company and the description matched nearly identical to what I had done before. It was the first post I saw where I thought *I can do that,* and felt confident about it. After some internal debate and discussion with Charlie I applied and waited to hear back. Could I do this? Did I want to do this? On one hand, I was totally terrified about the idea of going back to work. And on the other, I was excited about the possibility of doing more than just mom/wife/house work again. Milo was now two years old, and while he was still nursing, he was also walking and talking and eating plenty of table food. He would be OK if I left him during the day. And since Charlie wasn't working, I could leave him with his Dad, which helped as I always struggled with the idea of putting any of my children in daycare.

The company got back to me quickly. They scheduled a phone interview and then an in-person interview and next thing I knew I had a job offer! *Holy shit —I was going back to work!*

I was going to be working as a Junior Systems Administrator and my role would be nearly identical to what it had been six years prior. I would be responsible for a mix of Helpdesk support, systems maintenance, and updates. I would have the opportunity to implement new software to streamline the desktop setup. The company

was a global manufacturing company with offices all over the world, and they were desperately in need of more IT people. It was the perfect role for me.

I then had to quickly arrange afterschool care for Axel and Ethan. Charlie wouldn't be able to pick them up like I did because of the probation restrictions. He wasn't allowed on or near the school campus or anywhere where children hung out.

But, he could keep Milo with him and run errands and meal prep and do housework. I would just still have to manage the other day-to-day shuffling with the older two.

The weekend just before my new job started Morgan invited me out for her birthday. She wanted to get all her friends together for dinner and drinks. I hadn't been out with friends like that in what seemed like years so I decided to go.

At the party there was another mom who had two teenage kids. She was newly engaged to another one of my old coworkers, who was also friends with Morgan's husband Greg. I had met her a few times before but we had never talked very much. That night she told me the story of her children's father. He wasn't in their lives because he had been in prison for statutory rape of a 14-year-old when her kids were very young. She shared that for the first year he was in prison she stayed in the marriage and supported him. Her kids were babies at the time, and she didn't know or even believe she had the choice to leave.

She really wanted me to know that I could leave too. I didn't have to stay married to Charlie. I kept insisting I wanted to stay, that I loved him, and that I was supporting my family. All I could hear from her was disapproval and I was frustrated that she kept trying to get me to hear that it was OK to leave.

My intention had been to only stay for dinner and a

couple of drinks, but Morgan wanted to go to more bars afterwards. This was her kid-free night away too and she didn't want it to end. As soon as the liquor shots came out, Morgan pleaded with me to stay. I knew already at this point it wasn't safe to drive home, so I figured why not? We partied hard. Through my running, I had now lost over 50 pounds in weight, and the liquor hit me fast.

We ended up at a country bar and I had guys talking to me, clearly hitting on me, trying to get me to go somewhere with them. I was drunk enough to not know which way was up or really even what they were saying to me, but thankfully my other girl friends there swooped me back into their group on the dance floor.

At the next bar I started talking. I spilled the beans about the prostitutes that Charlie had admitted to seeing and that it was both men and women. I went on and on about the case and what he was up to. I aired all my dirty laundry to anyone else who could hear me. I was so intoxicated, and feeling like all the stories that I was hiding came spewing out and by letting them out, it allowed me a moment to finally breathe.

I ended up getting a safe ride home that night from another ex-coworker, the one now engaged to Morgan's friend who'd been through a similar situation as I was in. I hadn't seen him in years, but was grateful for the lift home. I stumbled into bed at 4am, completely smashed.

The next morning I was the sickest I have ever been after drinking. I was throwing up constantly, unable to stop. It was so bad, I nearly landed myself in the ER. Thankfully after throwing up every bite of food to get all the alcohol out of my stomach, it subsided and I was able to recover at home. No more girl's nights for me. It was time to focus on what was next.

I started my new job April 12, 2017—just under the one-year mark of Charlie's arrest. I was terrified that someone there was going to find out who he was, who I

was, but no one seemed to know anything. And if anyone did know, they certainly didn't bring it up to me.

I focused and jumped in head-first so I would get up to speed as quickly as I possibly could. I have always been a fast learner and I tend to integrate new technical concepts easily. This was no different. As scared as I was about the employment gap, it turned out the new versions of software worked nearly identical to the old ones. There were new features, but all the basic concepts were the same. I made customer service my priority and was the first to jump on every customer Helpdesk ticket. I made myself visible to others in a way I hadn't allowed myself to be for a long time.

I found myself enjoying being social again. My role meant regular interactions with nearly everyone there. People liked working with me, and I really appreciated feeling valued for something besides just being a mom.

The other thing that being at work meant was that I was no longer on the phone or physically around Charlie at all times. There was now a eight-to-nine hour period where my thoughts were my own. I had no idea the mental shift this was going to be for me, but it was huge. At first it was strange, and even uncomfortable. My mind was my own again—quiet even. Eventually I started to regain some sort of sovereignty over myself.

We all settled into a new routine with me working. I would get in my run in the morning before I went to work. Summer was approaching and so as soon as the kids were out of school I no longer had to take them and pick them up from school every day. It alleviated a huge weight for me to not have to be the kid chauffeur.

Charlie was excited to have the boys home with him all summer. They couldn't go to the playground, or do activities with other kids, but they could go for hikes, and play in the backyard. He was determined to make the most out of that summer together.

That August my little sister decided that she wanted to come for a visit to see me and the children. We didn't get to spend much time together during her wedding and she and I had been reconnecting more as she stepped into her newly married life.

She was going to be visiting for 10 days. I took a few days off of work, and we all were able to spend time together with the boys before they went back to school. My sister has always been more of a kid herself and loved playing LEGO® and games with the boys.

We also decided it would be fun to have some one-on-one sister time to take a drive through the mountain towns in Colorado. It was a beautiful drive, and she had never been through the area.

As we were driving it also gave us the chance to talk alone. She asked more about what had happened with Charlie's case. She had seen Charlie and I getting along, even being affectionate towards each other and she was confused. "He cheated on you, and you're totally fine?"

I tried to explain. I gave her the whole run down of what had happened in the case. I explained that I loved him and that he was working on himself. He was in sex offender treatment through the court. That everyone had demons, and at least now I knew what his were. I told her his side of the story that he wasn't trying to sleep with the 11 and 14-year-old, he was just trying to figure it out so he could report it.

She was understanding and compassionate. For the first time in a while I didn't feel judged for staying with him. She wanted to help if she could, but was careful not to insert her opinion about what I should or shouldn't do. She said she certainly didn't think she couldn't stay with someone who had cheated, but she also didn't know what it was like to have children with someone either.

I shared with her that the hardest part for me had been everyone's judgment. While I loved Charlie and

wanted to work on our marriage there was also a ton of shame around his offense. I felt isolated because there wasn't anyone I could talk to that would really get it.

She reminded me of our mom's journey with our dad and the parallels that ran through both of our stories. She thought I should try reaching out to our mom again, because she really could understand better than most people. I agreed to try.

After my sister went back home to Oregon, and I returned to work I felt the fog around me strengthen. I was truly terrified that anyone in my job would find out about Charlie's offense. I would not talk about my home life to ANYONE. I was so terrified that people were going to hear Charlie's name and connect my last name to him and what they read in the paper a year ago. Everyone at work knew I had a husband and children at home, but I never spoke about anything beyond the occasional kid antic. I kept that part of my life completely private. When I was home, I was in the family bubble. When I wasn't, the bubble didn't even exist.

I would happily prance around the office, chatting with everyone about work and life, helping with their computer problems, all the while never truly letting anyone see what was going on under the surface. I had created a level of safety away from what had happened and it was vital to me to keep that separation clear.

At the end of that year, the company Christmas party invitation sent me into a panic attack. People would expect my husband to come with me—right? Not only was I not sure he could get permission from probation to join, but I also wasn't even sure I wanted him to. An employee or spouse might recognize him—or learn his name. I could not have that come out. Work had become a sort of safe haven for me away from everything that Charlie had done. I had built some of an identity back. I also didn't want to hurt Charlie and tell him that. I was

stuck in between a rock and a hard place. I could not go? But I didn't want that either.

I ended up calling my mom to ask for her advice. I shared with her how I was feeling and wasn't sure what to do. She helped me see that it was totally fair to feel how I was feeling, and it didn't mean that I didn't support my husband. It was very easy for me to push aside my own feelings for others and in this case, I didn't think I could do that.

I ended up going to the Christmas party alone. Charlie was hurt, but on some level respected my need to keep his offense out of that part of my life. I just told my coworkers who asked that he ended up staying home with the kiddos.

My bubble was beginning to crumble. If I could not mix the two parts of my life, which one was the issue? The shame was all surrounding my home life, the fact that I stayed through all of that, and continued to be intimate in the marriage. It was weighing on me.

To make things worse, intimacy with Charlie had started to be more difficult. All of a sudden it felt like every escort he ever saw would be there in the room with us. Every time he looked at me affectionately, I would feel all of the other women and think, *Oh, that's how he looked at them.* I would get home and he would want to hear about my day, and I would not even want to look at him. I started drinking easily half a bottle of wine every night just to numb that feeling. What was happening to me?

I had no idea how to handle what was coming at me. My feelings were all over the place. My relationship with my kids was also suffering. They were with Charlie so much, it started to feel like I didn't even exist. I couldn't see what to do next. I didn't know how to fix it and get my family back.

To add even more to the confusion, I had started to build a strong sexual attraction to a coworker. His name

was Marcus and he had just gone through a breakup himself. It started out as innocent flirting, but it had begun escalating. I constantly fantasized about something happening between us at work after hours. I really wanted to explore what it would be like to be with someone who didn't bring their ghosts into the bedroom. Someone who didn't have the history that Charlie did. I wanted someone who wasn't my husband. *What the hell was I supposed to do with that?* I pushed it down and tried not to think about it. I had to focus on healing my marriage.

As a sex offender on probation, Charlie had an entirely different level of restrictions than people on regular probation. Sex offenders are not allowed contact with minors. Charlie's only exception was with his own children. Sex offenders are not allowed near schools, gyms, or anywhere where there might be children. Anything other than work, school, the grocery store, or home had to be by special request.

Because I was working and he was not, with the kids back in school, it was again very difficult to also be the one always dropping them off and picking them up. In order to get access to pick them up, we had to come up with a special request that would satisfy probation, his sex offender treatment therapist, as well as be approved by the school.

Sex offenders, at least in Colorado, are also regularly polygraphed as a way to determine if they are staying complaint with the restrictions. They're required to have two invasive sex history polygraphs before any leniency on their restrictions is given. As a way to try to get school pickups approved, Charlie was permitted to schedule those sooner than they normally would have been.

I was also going to be required to read these polygraphs because as his chosen safety person I had to be completely up to speed on everything in his history.

I took off one afternoon from work to meet Charlie at the therapist's office. The polygraph results weren't allowed to leave the office under any circumstances. The therapist also wanted to ensure that we could discuss the details afterwards together. I knew that reading these would be difficult, as I experienced a version of it before. What I didn't expect is yet another set of disclosures to come out.

This time the amount of prostitutes went from 50 to 100 over the time we were together. The number of infidelities literally doubled. Not only that, but there was admittance to a time in his teenage years when he found himself aroused by a toddler. His therapist watched me read the report. I was struggling and he knew it. He knew how important support people were in the lives of offenders, and yet I was not doing OK. The treatment team was completely unconcerned about the report and told us that they would likely be able to approve the safety plan for Charlie to pick up the children as long as the school agreed. *What? This is considered good?* I mean, he was the professional. Again, I shoved it all down. I mean, I got what I wanted...right?

To distract myself from my feelings, I continued to pour myself into work. Now that I could, I started staying late most nights, just wanting to not have to be around Charlie. Marcus, who was not in a rush to go home to an empty house, would join me most of the time. I pretended I was just a committed employee, when really I still was very much fantasizing about what might happen between us.

It seemed like a bad idea on so many levels. I mean I was married, and we were coworkers. I was about to mix my two worlds in about as messy of a way as possible. Why I felt the need to sabotage literally everything, I have no clue. But the feelings only grew and I got to the point where this was clearly a force beyond my control

and this was going to happen.

I decided that since I knew what it felt like to be cheated on, I was not going to do it in secret. I was going to come out and tell Charlie how I felt and where I was at. I knew he could feel that things weren't good with me and hadn't been for a while. I knew he noticed the drinking and the distance. But he was not going to be expecting this.

I was so ashamed and terrified at the same time. I was ashamed that now I was the one wanting to step outside of the marriage. *I mean, seriously Amanda, what the fuck? After everything we'd just been through?* I was terrified of being responsible for the breakup of the family. I didn't think we could remain living together—what would that mean for the kids? He was still on sex offender probation. I took on ALL of the possibilities and the outcomes as my responsibility. Even with that weighing at me, staying together was not an option anymore.

As women we tend to take on the responsibility of holding the family together. Men were allowed and at some points in time even expected to travel, go to war, visit brothels—it was all considered normal. Women had the role of the house, the family, the children—we were the glue that held the family together. And if we were the glue, then when the family unit collapsed, it was all our fault.

I am and was a very independent woman who did not prescribe to that patriarchal bullshit. And yet— that's exactly how I felt. I was making the choice to collapse this all. But like I said, there seemed to be a force bigger than me, guiding me here—and I was not capable of stopping myself either.

Marcus was just as frustrated with his own life and said to me as he was leaving the office one evening, "Everything wrong in your life has one common denominator. You can't blame anyone else but yourself."

I was triggered so hard. *WAIT, I'm not responsible for THIS?!?*

It set me off and I spilled the beans about Charlie, about the arrest, about my struggle to be in the marriage. All of it.

"I am not responsible for THIS."

I shocked him with all of it, but he listened to my story as it poured out of me. After that he looked at me differently. Not with pity, but with a kind of respect that I hadn't been expecting. "You went through all that, are still going through it, AND you show up here to the office kicking ass every day?"

I was not expecting him to respond like that, but I appreciated the recognition. The doorway had officially been opened between us.

Our after work conversations continued. He tried to help me see other possibilities for things I could do. He let me vent about my frustrations, everything that I had been bottling up inside. He listened to how difficult it had been for me, the restrictions, the isolation, the feeling like I had no choice but to stay in my marriage. I couldn't kick my children's father out on the street—that was unacceptable.

At the same time I got to know him more too. He had been with his last girlfriend for five years, and he was broken up with in a pretty shitty way. He was struggling emotionally, and was in his own way very depressed. He lived alone, no pets, very few friends, nothing else but his job to keep him going.

And while he liked the people we worked with, he really struggled with our boss and the management at the company. He felt stifled and under appreciated. Our boss was my age, which was 13 years younger than Marcus was. Marcus felt our boss didn't know how many of the systems worked, and usually caused more harm to operations than he helped.

I just listened to him. I had a different relationship with our boss, and with management myself. I got a lot of kudos for my work and relationship building, but I also agreed that was not how Marcus experienced them.

More often than not after work, we were the last two people there. Now that Charlie could pick up the boys, there was no hurry for me to go back home. I really didn't even want to be home anymore. I missed my children, but there was no way to spend time with them without Charlie.

I let myself believe that my new friendship was harmless and I could just keep a handle on the rest of my feelings, at least for the time being, until I could figure out what I really wanted.

Chapter 10

Every winter in Durango the town hosts a massive street party called Snowdown to celebrate. There are tons of events, games, and competitions. Every year there is a new theme and everyone dresses up and participates. This year it was "A Black Tie Affair." Everyone was going to be wearing formal clothes, and fancy dresses.

My company also sponsored one of the events, a spelling bee. As a sponsor we had a table of contestants and every year, the other employees were encouraged to go in support. I decided I wanted to go and convinced Marcus to come with me. I bought the most revealing provocative, glitter sequin dress I could find. I even shaved my nether regions for the first time in years. I fully intended to make it blatantly obvious that I was interested. I could easily blame the alcohol while still getting an idea of where he stood.

Marcus was no dummy and caught on to my flirtations right away. He made jokes about making sure I got home safely. After the event was over we walked around town and checked out a couple more events. I caught him checking out my backside and I smiled at him.

I went home knowing that things were escalating far from just friendship. I was still totally scared about what was coming, but also completely excited about the possibilities.

The next week at work after everyone left, Marcus said to me, "You better decide exactly what it is you want from me before we get drunk together again."

I looked him directly in the eyes and responded "What can I have?"

"Whatever you want."

Damn. It was on.

February 6th was Charlie and my wedding an-niversary. Eight years together. He sent me a massive vase of flowers to the office. Like this thing was bigger than my whole upper body. The receptionist called me to come get them and I had to use a dang computer cart to move them to my office. I could barely fit my arms around it.

I knew this was Charlie's way of celebrating, but truthfully I was so embarrassed to still be in the marriage and the way I reacted to that embarrassment was anger. I saw the flowers and immediately my emotions went red. I was so flipping pissed. *HOW FUCKING DARE HE!?* I felt like Charlie was claiming me like a dog peeing on a tree in front of the whole office staff. I intentionally kept him far away from my work and so he pulled this? I was fuming and also could not exactly explain to anyone what on earth I was so upset about.

That evening I went home on time. Our anniversary evening was fairly normal. As I always did, I stuffed down my anger and frustration and tried to be nice. He wanted to try to go out to dinner, and I really didn't feel up to it. I felt like I was going to burst if I got pushed any harder. I told him the size of the flowers embarrassed me, and it was really not necessary. He knew I didn't like to talk about him at work. I really didn't want anyone to know who he was. He knew how much I wanted to keep his offense out of my job.

I also knew it was time to tell him what was going on with me, but today didn't seem like the day to do it either.

After the kids were in bed, Charlie handed me another present. A small box. I opened it to find a stunning diamond ring. An engagement ring. I'm confused, so he explained. When we got married eight years ago he was adamant that I was not going to have a

diamond ring. He wanted only "equal" bands. In his previous two marriages (I was wife #3) he had always felt like the ring was a sign of not being equal and was used somehow in a way he didn't like. I eventually agreed to no diamonds, but never liked it. I'm a bit of a girly girl and I do like pretty things, and so I wanted a ring. And yet, I recognized, the husband himself was more important than jewelry.

So this change of heart set off emotions in me that I didn't know were still there. I was transported back in time 10 years before when that's all I would have wanted from him. Recognition of me and my desires. Wanting to buy me something pretty just because I would enjoy it. Feeling cared for and wanted. I saw us 10 years ago, at the beginning of it all. Before all this had happened, before kids, before everything.

I missed us. I had been struggling to find it again, but here it was. Charlie and I kissed and it felt good. We slept together for the first time in a long time, and I felt more connected than I could ever remember us being. This was what I had been searching for.

I didn't know it at the time, but this would be the last time Charlie and I would have sex.

The next morning I woke up confused again. What the fuck am I going to do now? I didn't want to wear the ring. I didn't want to wear any wedding ring anymore. I went to work to face Marcus.

The moment I saw Marcus I knew that the previous night with Charlie had changed nothing. That person I was 10 years ago, wasn't me anymore. It was time to tell Charlie the truth. I didn't want to wait long either, that wasn't fair to anyone.

I was so scared to talk to him. He thought things were great now. A couple days later I finally worked up the nerve to send him a text while I sat on the living room couch and he was in the other room. We often texted

things rather than talking in front of the kids, and if I didn't do it now, I was sure I'd lose my nerve. I told him the truth. That I knew what being cheated on felt like so I wanted to be honest. That the me who wanted that ring wasn't me anymore. I wasn't happy and hadn't been for awhile. That I was interested in someone else and wanted to pursue it.

He was shocked and hurt to say the least. He wanted to know more, and I didn't give him any details. I told him the guy was interested too, but nothing had happened yet. I wanted to tell him first. I gave him back the ring, and said I couldn't accept it.

Phew, wow, OK I did it. Hard as that was to admit to myself, it was even harder to admit to Charlie. There was no going back now.

Now, I was ready. I wanted Marcus, and I wanted him bad. And now that Marcus knew it, there was no stopping it. That weekend he sent me a text that said, "Come over" and a Google Maps location of his house. It shocked me so hard, I nearly dropped the phone. I wanted to go so badly, but I had literally just told Charlie a couple days ago. I tried to tell him I was going. He begged and pleaded with me not to. He begged me to work on our marriage instead. He knew he didn't really get a say after what he did, but he still wanted me. We went in circles for hours. I ended up not going, but never wavered on my desire.

The next Monday after work, it was just me and Marcus left in the office. We hadn't talked about his invitation all day. It was now only two days before Valentine's Day, and I was packing my stuff to get ready to leave. I had my bags on my shoulder and we both were headed to the door. Marcus looked at me with intense desire in his eyes and walked towards me instead of the door. We both dropped our things, and our mouths met. It was immediately electric. My entire body was

vibrating. I couldn't remember ever feeling a desire that intense. My mouth and my body were all over his. *Holy shit what was happening?* We pulled away both out of breath and both in some kind of shock. *What the fuck was that?* I knew if we didn't leave we wouldn't be able to stop ourselves from going further right then and there.

That Valentine's Day Marcus and I got together. He saw how sad I was that it was Valentine's Day and invited me out for a drink. We chatted for a while, both only having one thing on our minds. We finished one drink each, intending to go home right after. He walked me to my car, both saying no we aren't going to do this, we're coworkers and all that, it's a bad idea. And at the same time we were not able to keep our hands off each other. After another intensely electric kiss in front of my car, he told me his parent's summer house was empty, and it was only five minutes away. I agreed to follow him there, knowing exactly what was about to happen. I felt alive. I was not a burden to him; I was an excitement.

Being with Marcus reawakened me sexually in a way I hadn't felt in a long time with Charlie. I had never had this type of immediate electric connection with someone before. Not only that but there were no ghosts or secrets jumping out at me.

After that, Charlie only tried harder to convince me to stay with him. I came home after work to a letter he wrote me sitting on the counter. It was four pages long. I started to read it as he finished cooking dinner.

He called it "Admissions and Apologies." It began by him admitting to all the things that hurt me throughout our relationship. He was not only admitting to what happened, but he was admitting to doing so *knowing* that these things would hurt me, and callously still doing them anyway.

He admitted to being unfaithful when we first started dating. He knew I loved him and would have done almost

anything for him. He admitted to lying to me and telling me what I wanted to hear about ending things with his previous wife, and then dragging it out with her, while also still seeing me.

He admitted to lying to me about being committed to me when we got married. He admitted to not sharing his thoughts or any other area of his life with me. He admitted to keeping me away from hearing about any part of his day. He admitted to using my own insecurities to make sure that I never felt good enough to be included in other areas of his life.

He admitted to never asking me about how I was doing, or being there for me. He admitted to allowing "good enough" to be a successful partnership.

He admitted that when we became parents he wanted me to stay home with the babies, but then let me feel guilty for financially depending on him. He admitted to never helping me create more time or energy for myself, only doing the bare minimum to help with the house or children, while still wanting all of my attention for himself. He admitted to representing himself as a good father, while barely ever being present.

He admitted that he still expected me to be available to him for comfort, for conversation, and for sex despite always distracting himself with other things. If I interrupted what he was doing, he became annoyed with me, using my imperfections to excuse his behavior.

He admitted to never calling or coming home when he knew I wanted to spend time together, putting himself above me. He admitted to feeling sorry for himself, rather than ever trying to make the effort to hear what I was saying.

He admitted to never being willing to participate in activities with me or the family, even while claiming to want them.

He admitted to using pornography that I would not

approve of, knowing that I would be unlikely to nag or try to control him and ask him to stop. He admitted to using pornography and masturbation as a way to avoid intimacy and connection.

He admitted to fantasizing and fetishizing my teenage promiscuous past. He admitted to asking me to do sex acts with others after I clearly said I was not interested.

He admitted to going outside of our marriage to have sex with others. He admitted to putting my health and the children's health at risk. He admitted to breaking my trust and lying while also representing himself as innocent and trustworthy. He admitted to maliciously giving away the physical intimacy of the marriage to others.

He admitted to doing this not 10 or even 50 times, but repeatedly and with callousness.

He admitted to abusing the prostitutes. He admitted to telling himself they were OK so he could feel OK with what he was doing. He admitted to pretending he was just a nice guy helping them. He admitted to ignoring my calls while he was with them.

He admitted to degrading himself, cursing me, and bringing the ghosts of all of the others he was with into our bedroom.

He admitted to meeting underage girls for sex. He admitted to crossing every single line that exists through the process of being arrested, jailed, charged, and convicted. He admitted to thinking he was slick enough to not get caught. He admitted to considering doing even worse things.

He admitted to continuing to play the victim. He admitted to using his mental health to gain pity from me and others. He admitted to allowing me to consider if I was somehow to blame, and then pretending to take full responsibility without ever actually doing so.

He admitted to minimizing every single frustration or concern I ever had. If that wasn't what he meant for me to feel, then it was not his fault that I was upset.

He admitted to comparing his crime against all those women and children to me dating someone new.

He admitted to lying repeatedly and deliberately. He admitted to knowing the whole time exactly what he was doing. And still doing it anyway.

He then apologized for it all. For diminishing me and our family. He commited to remain diligent about his demons.

And still after saying all of that, he was not done. He proceeded to ask for me to stay with him. He was arrogant enough to believe that I still loved him, and wanted him. He asked for me to accept more struggle and pain after everything that he had done, just to be with him. He asked me to again risk being hurt and broken.

He asked me to believe that he has changed and can change. He asked me to believe that he could be the person for me, to challenge me, love me, push me, and believe in me. That he was the one person who can truly bring me happiness after all of this.

He acknowledged that I had a few nice moments with someone else, and there was a part of him that knew that's what I needed, to be with someone that doesn't have ghosts in the bedroom. But he wouldn't apologize for wanting me, and telling me over and over.

He asked for me, all of me, in return for all of him. He eventually will ask for my monogamy, but he said that wasn't his priority right then. He had too much work to do on himself right then. He wanted forever, not just tomorrow.

As I stood there at the kitchen counter reading every word, every admission, every place where my heart broke throughout our marriage, I knew that it was truly

over between us. I was done. He was never the man I thought he was. He thought that by admitting his faults and wrongdoings that I could forgive him and come back to him. But what he did instead was show me that he was maliciously cold and calculating. He knew what sleeping with escorts would do to me. He knew and did it anyway. He showed me that he always knew how I felt and the connection I wanted with him, but instead of connecting with me, he intentionally used my insecurities to his advantage. He showed me that he'd always known exactly what he was doing.

I set the paper down and went into my bedroom. I texted him, asking again not to have the conversation in front of the children. "I'm done. I want you to move out of my bedroom now."

I was livid. More mad than I ever was before. *Screw him.* He again tried to stop me, talk to me. He would not let me out of his sight. He began chasing me around the house pleading with me to change my mind. I went into the bedroom, outside, anywhere I could think of and he followed me. I just wanted to get away from him and he would not let up. I started getting scared. I could not leave a room without him following me. He would not stop pleading and begging me to see things differently. There was no escape. I ran and locked myself in the bathroom and he banged on the door.

He sat outside of it sobbing and yelling at me to listen to him. To give us a chance. I told him to go away. Leave me alone.

I even texted Marcus, as I didn't know what to do. I felt trapped in my own house. Marcus suggested calling the cops. I didn't want to do that, there was no physical violence here. So, I just hid. I figured he'd eventually go away.

Charlie did eventually give up, and left me alone. He slept in another room that night, and started moving his

things out of the master bedroom the next day while I was at work.

When I got to work the next morning, Marcus handed me a set of keys. Keys to his parent's house and keys to his house. Just in case I needed an escape. He needed me to know I always had a safe place to go. It was a gesture that I didn't expect, and I was truly more grateful than I could say.

Things calmed down for a while after that. Charlie decided what he needed was a project and so he decided to remodel the downstairs to create a new master suite for himself. He still refused to move out, but didn't want to keep sleeping on the boy's floor either. He focused on that new project while I focused on Marcus.

Chapter 11

Despite my roller coaster of a marriage, and being coworkers, my relationship with Marcus flourished. We couldn't get enough of each other. We kept quiet at the office, but we went to music shows, on mini road trips, and went camping together. All of a sudden, I was allowed to have fun again. I could be free in my own body, away from everything that the last year had been. Marcus loved making me smile. When I told my mom about him I said, "He makes my smile muscles hurt!" And it was true! I had never laughed before like I did with him. Being with Marcus allowed me to forget everything that was happening at home and that was something I needed so badly.

My mom came to visit us that summer. It was the first time she saw us since the arrest. We had continued reconnecting over regular phone calls and it had now been two years since she'd seen the boys. I wasn't entirely sure how the visit would go after last time, but I was also hopeful that maybe some of the relationship could be repaired.

I think sometimes it takes going through your own big stuff as an adult to see what your parents went through more clearly. It's not easy as a child to see the bigger picture. Until then, I could not see what happened in my childhood clearly either.

Marcus thought it would be great if we scheduled more outings and activities with my mom. Rather than sit around the house, having excursions planned would make everyone's experience more exciting and also bring less opportunity for conflict. So I did just that. I scheduled a Jeeping trip through the mountains— something I'd never done before. We made plans to go to

her favorite hot springs, visit mesa verde national park, and go to the recreation center pool. I was only able to take a couple days off of work, but I could make the most of those days.

When my mom got there everyone was in good spirits. Charlie was gracious to her and my stepdad, and Marcus came over to meet them as well. My mom immediately took to Marcus, which truly surprised me. She never liked anyone I dated.

Marcus came with us on the Jeeping trip, while Charlie watched the boys. I drove the whole time through the mountains and had a blast. I don't think I'd had that much fun with my mom in over a decade. I was so grateful for the opportunity.

That evening Marcus stayed over and he and my mom sat outside and talked. He shared with her how he felt about me, and how important it was to him to make sure I always had a safe place to go. He told her how amazing he thought I was, and how well I was kicking butt at work. My mom just adored Marcus. He was talkative and very transparent with her about his feelings for me. That meant so much to her, especially after what we'd all been through.

The next evening, after Marcus had gone home, this time it was Charlie and her that talked. He knew she was around two years ago, although they didn't see each other then as he was just out on bond. He told her his side of the story, and what he was working on in his treatment program. She is a licensed therapist who worked with addicts for years and knows a lot about the various methodologies for rehabilitation.

She asked him some questions, but generally let him talk. She was cautious but thanked him for his willingness to share.

The next day she and I had scheduled time for just her and I to drive to the hot springs an hour away. I

couldn't remember the last time we had spent time together just the two of us. It was long overdue and I was excited to spend the day together. I shared more about how the relationship with Marcus started, and how much I was enjoying feeling joyful again. She shared more of her own journey with divorcing my dad and what she learned about herself from that experience.

It was like I could finally see her as a mom who was really just trying to do the very best she could. She had to take care of herself in order to take care of us. After my dad hit her, she didn't feel safe around him, and didn't trust him around us. *Boy, did I understand that now.* She said she had tried to work with him in the courts, but he refused to get help with his anger and refused to set up a normal house for us to visit him in. She didn't want us staying overnight on his 20-foot boats—they didn't even have bathrooms—it made no sense.

She also shared that while she appreciated Charlie's disclosure, as a mental health professional and someone who has been incredibly sensitive and intuitive her whole life, she had some big concerns about Charlie's treatment program. She recognized the methods they were using and from her lensing, they rarely were successful long-term. She told me that when Charlie spoke there was deep darkness behind his eyes. She didn't know what the darkness was, but it unsettled her. She felt there was a lot more under the surface than we'd seen yet.

While I knew she was right, I had no clue what to do about it. What kind of darkness was in him? I'd seen how he reacted to our separation, but I had no idea what else might be there. For the moment, I was just going to have to stay aware and see what else unfolded.

Things with Marcus continued through the summer. There were weeks where I spent one or two nights with him, and weeks where I didn't see him at all outside of work. While we adored each other, we also didn't quite

know how to navigate a relationship where I was still married, we were working closely together, and I had small children. Both of us were completely conflict avoidant and totally stubborn about reaching out if things got a little weird.

Charlie also really did not want to move out—in fact he pushed hard to stay in the house so we could "keep the family together." He pulled on all of my obligatory strings and fears about blowing up the boy's world again. So here I was dating a coworker while living with my spouse and children. Just a tad bit messy. Marcus would come over to the house and no one knew how to act. Charlie literally never left the house, and so if I needed to be away from him, I also had to be away from my children.

We started examining what the living situation might morph into. I wanted more space and distance, but neither of us wanted time away from the children. We researched options other families had done—some living very close together. Others even built houses that allowed for shared spaces and not shared spaces.

Charlie started house shopping. Our current home didn't have a great way to do much to change the layout, and he thought maybe we could find something that would allow for more space for everyone. He had nearly completed the remodel of downstairs to create a new bedroom for himself but there was no separate entrance and no separate living spaces.

He found a house he liked that had been already redone to have two master suites. One original, and one with a separate entrance but still connected to the main house. We went to look at it, and both of us could see how it would work. If I had Marcus over, he wouldn't even have to interact with the family if we didn't want to—but the kids could find me if they needed me. And if Charlie wanted space, he had a master area that would be

separate from any of my spaces. Shared spaces would include kitchen, dining, and living areas, and the kids rooms would all be together in the middle.

Charlie got really excited about the idea and wanted to make an offer. I was unsure about it. I didn't know that it would solve anything but I also knew what we had going on now wasn't working either. I eventually agreed to make an offer. We signed the papers and he went in to hand the realtor the deposit check.

The next day Charlie got a call from his probation officer. Someone had called and reported Charlie for trying to move into the neighborhood. They didn't like that he was going to live close to the elementary school in the area. In Colorado, there are no laws limiting where sex offenders can live, but as an offender on sex offender probation he was not permitted to make any type of big financial or moving decisions without approval from his supervisory team. So the call was essentially to say he was in violation of probation, and would have to go through a corrective action plan.

Now, that seems like a big deal but really it wasn't as far as the impact to Charlie. He'd have to discuss the impact and complete some homework assignments, but it was fairly minimal. But to me, this was a massive red flag. Someone within 24 hours of us going under contract for a new home, called probation to report on him. I could only assume it was the sellers themselves or someone in the realtors office. We hadn't told anyone else our plans.

I was livid. Terrified really. All of my fight or flight responses activated just like they did when that first newspaper article came out. I wanted out and I wanted nothing to do with any real estate deal. I was NOT OK doing business with anyone who would report him to probation. My children were going to be living here and going to school here. It made me so uncomfortable

knowing that we were being watched like that. Fortunately the relator hadn't deposited the check, and so we were able to cancel the contract.

We took a big step back and decided it was not yet time to look at other living options.

At this point, Charlie was also trying to be friends with Marcus. He would go out of his way to make dinner for all of us if he knew he was coming over after work. Charlie even confided in us that he was romantically interested in one of the other men in his therapy group. He'd been spending time with him socially, and had developed an attraction. It was a bit odd, but he seemed to be moving on from me, and so on one hand I was happy that he for a moment was not obsessing about me. And yet on the other hand, dating another sex offender meant he may want to bring him around the children.

He brought his new friend over for me to meet and get to know him a bit. Charlie was still just crushing on him, and hadn't yet told him how he felt. He was a nice enough guy, and shared Charlie's love for mountain biking, not to mention he was attractive, so I could see why Charlie was interested. He was a contractor and had helped some with ideas for the basement renovation project. Later when I asked for details beyond what the internet said about his offense, I wasn't given any. Thankfully he refused Charlie's advances, and after that, I never saw him again.

None of Charlie or my own ideas of a new normal lasted. As much as we all tried on this idea of weird family arrangements, it just didn't make any sense. The boys didn't actually understand what was going on. At the same time, as long as the adults acted normal, they just went along with it. I'm certain it was actually quite confusing for them on some level, as it certainly was for all of us. I refused to let myself see it as I really wanted some version of happiness for them, but I couldn't figure

out what that could be anymore.

It took me some time to realize what was starting to happen. My kids were no longer seeing me in the same lens they always had. Charlie began telling them that I was leaving THEM. That programming was being planted and it was coming out in their behavior towards me.

We got Axel into play therapy as he was the one with the most questions and having the most difficulty with what was going on. My hope was to make a relationship with a therapist so we could start to form more of an understanding for them regarding what Charlie's offense was actually about. The amount of family changes the children were experiencing were starting to take its toll.

Milo, who was now three, asked me one day if I was going to have another baby and move away from them. "What? Why would you ask that?" No three-year-old comes up with that idea on their own.

But what could I do? I was not remotely interested in a romantic relationship with Charlie anymore. I was starting to finally see the manipulations for what they were. He blamed me for stepping out of the marriage, but why did I do that? Why was I disconnected? I was disconnected after finally starting to process that my husband had cheated on me more than 100 times. Kind of a no brainer, right? I was angry that this was being turned against me, and I was at a loss of how to get back in control of what was starting to unfold.

I went to a lawyer for advice. I knew things were not going to stay OK for much longer, but I wasn't sure if it was time to make the jump or not. She essentially confirmed my suspicions. Having supported him at all ever, was going to be a barrier for me to overcome if I was going to go down this path. The more he painted himself as the stay-at-home dad, the more the court would see that I trusted him as a parent.

I still believed that he was a good dad. The boys loved him dearly. Manipulative as fuck, yes, but that was my problem not theirs. Or so I thought.

I did nothing for a long time. I didn't want to make things even worse. That summer the boys were home with Charlie instead of doing summer camp. Again because of the restrictions, either I had to take them to a full-time camp, or they had to be home. There was no middle option with my work hours. Their behavior also worsened. They became combative towards me and towards each other. They acted like I was no longer their mother—I was just someone who came over sometimes. Milo still would come snuggle in bed with me at night, but mostly he followed whatever his brothers did.

My job was still a safe place for me, and I was gaining increasing responsibility there. I had already been promoted IT Project Manager and I was doing so well there that I was offered the IT Manager position in August of 2018. Trouble was, now I was going to be Marcus's boss, and that was a big no-no. I decided that as hard as it was, it was time to end that relationship. Things had been getting more and more difficult as I kept being pulled in two directions. Knowing that the more time I spent with Marcus, the more ammunition it gave Charlie to alienate the children. He had told the kids that I had essentially chosen Marcus over them. It was time to choose them.

Ending the relationship really, really sucked. He was pissed that I didn't even give him a say about anything or even have a conversation about it—I just decided. I knew that if I let him talk, I would cave, and I didn't want to do that. It was time to focus on my job and my kids and put my life back together in some fashion. I was so grateful for what Marcus brought to me and helped remind me of. He had helped me find the parts of me that had been long gone. Finding carefree fun and joy again was a gift I

was so grateful for, but now it was time to move forward.

We did remain friends. Once the hurt wore off, we both decided that being in each other's lives as good friends was better than being distant coworkers or not being friends at all. And yes, there were still many innuendos and some not so subtle flirting, but I was firm that there was a line we were not crossing. I had to get my shit together and fast.

The house next door came up for sale and Charlie suggested buying it. He knew I still needed more space, and he still didn't want to be far from the kids. I wasn't sure at first. I was still pretty raw from the last round, but the more I thought about it, the easier it seemed this time. I had an intense job, and sometimes might need help. This might be a way to get him to actually move sooner. And this time I wouldn't be moving with him. The existing neighbors already knew whatever they knew. We decided to go for it. We offered cash, an easy and fast sale. The plan was that Charlie would move out slowly as he got the new place setup, and the transition would be as smooth as it could be for everyone. At least that was my understanding.

But as soon as I ended things with Marcus, Charlie then took that as an opening to start trying to get back together with me again. I was not remotely interested. In fact, I became disgusted by what he had been doing and the games he was playing with me and the kids. I still struggled with HOW exactly to begin to split households though. I didn't want to be away from my kids half the time. I wanted to reconnect with them. I wanted Charlie to leave so I could do that, but he wouldn't even leave for one night. Even after the house sale was completed, he still wouldn't move. And now I had no escape to Marcus's either. I needed him out of my house NOW.

He didn't let up easily. I got provocative love letters and emails declaring his love for me. He would insist on

trying to hug me before work even when I was clear that I did not want him to touch me. He would push and push and I kept holding the boundary firm. It was exhausting and truly maddening.

He seemed to think that if he just said the right thing I would wake up and realize I loved him and run back to him. He could not understand that he was not entitled to me just because he wanted me. He would start to realize his negative behavior after the fact, but he could never seem to actually figure out how to change it. I would just get the sob story about how sorry he was and how much work he needed to do. *No shit, dude.*

I tried to reach out to his therapist for support. His therapist agreed with me that the letters and advances were inappropriate especially given the state of our relationship. I didn't know who else to ask for help from and I only hoped they could help him see his behavior.

Charlie must have felt threatened again with where it was all heading because that October, he handed me divorce paperwork. He said he didn't want to be with someone who didn't want him anymore. This was a total 180 from his prior stance and it threw me again. He all of a sudden wanted to get the courts involved. Why? He was the one with the felony; it made no sense to me. When I had spoken to my lawyer, she had said there may be some judges who wouldn't give him custody even if I agreed to it with what he had done. I didn't know whether that was true or not, but why would he risk it?

When divorce papers are filed each party is now no longer able to make big financial decisions or leave the state with the children. I had scheduled a trip with the boys to go to my sister's house for Thanksgiving that November, and all of a sudden I was going to need written permission to go. Tickets were already bought and my mom and step-dad were also planning on meeting us all there.

I immediately asked Charlie for permission to go and he refused to give it to me. He thought he should have been invited to go, and I shouldn't have purchased tickets in the first place. He was digging in his heels trying to block me from seeing my family.

I found out what else he was up to a week later. He had also filed a temporary orders document claiming he was the primary parent, and to keep continuity for the children *I* was the one who should move out. He wanted me to move into the house we just bought for him!? No fucking way. I was so angry I literally saw red. *After what he did—he wanted ME to leave? HE was the primary parent? What the ever-loving fuck is going on here?*

He wanted to play hard ball. He wanted to push his weight around. It was a massive power and control dynamic and I was not having it at all. I had to figure out how to start fighting back.

What was interesting here is that for me this was ANOTHER betrayal. After everything I did to support him and the family, this was how he repaid me? It was like the moment the fog lifted for me, and I started to wake up, he saw that as an opportunity to go on attack. I was devastated that this was where we ended up. I didn't want to be with him, but I wanted my family to be OK. I needed my kids to be OK—and I had no idea how to make that happen.

When I went back to work and became less available, my friend Morgan, the same one who helped me so much when he was first arrested, started texting Charlie daily, and they began to develop a closer friendship of sorts. Their friendship made me uncomfortable and so I distanced myself more from her because of it. I wasn't sure if it was romantic or not, but she had also just filed for divorce from her husband, Greg, and I knew she was using herself as primary parent to get him moved out, and so I assumed that Charlie was just following suit.

This is a common technique used in the family court system. One parent tries to establish dominance because as soon as the courts identify who that primary parent is —it's really hard to undo. The person staying in the family home more often than not is seen as that person, and that was why he was so adamant it be him. In our case it made zero sense as Charlie couldn't even go to the children's schools or activities. He couldn't be around any of their friends. He was a felony sex offender trying to claim he was their primary parent. It was so convoluted.

I pushed over and over to get permission to go see my family, and eventually as he was spending an afternoon over at Morgan's house, he sent me a text allowing me to take the boys on the trip. He had been trying to make me feel extremely guilty about it but it wasn't working. I was grateful that we were going to be getting a few days away from the turmoil.

The trip to Portland was very different this time. My mom and stepdad, sister, and brother-in-law were all staying in my sister's new house which had enough room for everyone, including me and the boys. We spent more time together, doing activities the boys would enjoy. I continued running daily and making sure I was still taking care of my mental health. We even made sure to call Charlie every night so he could say goodnight to the boys. I wasn't trying to exclude him from their life, but I no longer wanted him in mine.

When we got back, the accusations continued. He was hurt and lashing out at me. He started excluding me in the regular family activities. I felt like I was living in a war zone.

Part of me even started to feel like maybe I was actually doing something wrong. Charlie always had a way of talking to me like he knew something I didn't. There was some hidden agenda there that was lurking waiting to jump out. The fear reaction in me started

rising—what was this man actually capable of? He would get this smirk on his face when he thought he had you. There was an evil behind it and it made you just want to scream. He would bring up all sorts of unrelated things that he felt I did wrong and twist them to his narrative. According to him, even me going back to work was abandoning the children.

I didn't know how to react to these accusations. He would tell me I was a narcissist and selfish for what I was doing. I never really tried to save the marriage, everything was all pretending. He would never allow me to even walk away from a conversation with him. If I tried to end it, he would follow me around the house getting one more word in. If I didn't answer he would stand there impatiently staring at me, trying to get me to engage. Shutting doors only escalated to screaming. I had no way to reclaim my sense of self.

There was one evening the boys were downstairs watching TV and he started talking about all the ways I'd hurt him and what I had done wrong. I just sat and listened. I didn't get up, knowing he'd follow me if I did. I thought if I just stayed quiet, he'd stop. But he didn't. He went on and on and on. How Morgan had told him things I said about him, and he knew what I was really up to. How I just couldn't help myself—the first man who gave me attention I jumped on. Morgan told him how I was making out with some guys at the bar on her birthday night, long before we broke up. How I was such a horrible human for doing all of this to the family. My whole body began shaking in fear and he just continued. He went on for over an hour, never noticing that I was in distress. I kept quiet and just took the beating. I sat there shaking uncontrollably while I was verbally and emotionally assaulted. I could not move to get away even if I wanted to.

Eventually the boys came upstairs and wanted food and he stopped talking. I got up and left the room. He needed to leave NOW. I texted his family asking them to help me get him out. No response from any of them. I even texted Marcus—*what do I do?* He told me to call the cops. I was so scared that they would escalate if I did. Eventually his family got a hold of him and talked him into leaving for the night. The moment he left was the first time I took a deep breath in months. That's when I knew that there was more to this man than I ever understood. There was something deeply wrong here. My body had been trying to tell me I wasn't safe, and I hadn't been listening. I was going to have to find a way to protect myself and my children. It was not going to be easy, but dammit, I had to try.

Chapter 12

From the time the temporary orders request was filed, it was a six week wait until court. Six weeks of living in the same house, tiptoeing around each other. Charlie was playing Dad as hard as he could. I'd come home from work and they'd already have eaten dinner, and were doing an activity. I wasn't a welcome part of their group. He would schedule outings to see his family and not tell me. I was a stranger in my own home.

Those six weeks felt like an eternity. I would hide out in my room as much as I could after the kids went to bed. I tried to engage with them in activities on the weekend like taking them to the pool or playground or museums. Charlie couldn't come to those activities with other kids around, so it was all I could do to have alone time with my children. Charlie would want all the details of where we were going every time before he'd permit us to even leave the house. He made sure the boys wore their GPS cellular watches so he could track our location. I'm not sure if he thought I was going to run away with them or what, but it was crazy-making.

At this point I wasn't sure what he was or wasn't hiding. His behavior was erratic and increasingly paranoid. One day when he left to go for a bike ride, I decided to search his room. I really didn't know what I'd find, but I thought it was worth a quick peek. I opened his closet and there was a pile of paperwork. Safety plans mostly for probation. I found one that he wrote about moving next door—clearly he had indeed always known that we bought that house for him. I took a photo of that one for court. I also found a new one where he asked to begin dating. Interesting from a man who claimed to want to stay together. The next document was more

intriguing. It was a violation notice from probation stating Charlie had been reprimanded for a "pattern of minor violations." What on earth did this mean? I took another photo. My heart was racing and I decided that this was entirely a bad idea to keep digging, so I closed the closet and left.

A pattern of minor violations? These felt an awful lot like the boundary pushing he'd been doing with me. I'd witnessed him pushing probation's boundaries too. He would often go outside in the street with the boys while they were playing with the neighbor kids—while seemingly harmless, as a man on sex offender probation, it was not. He was very clearly ordered not to have ANY contact whatsoever with any minor. He did versions of this all the time. Just stepping right up to the boundary line and pushing it just a bit to see if it was still there. It was the same behavior he would do with me when I told him I didn't want to be in the relationship anymore. Touching me, giving me gifts, hugging me without permission, and sending me all kinds of explicit love notes.

Charlie wasn't gone long, and when he got home, he went into his room and then immediately stormed upstairs. I was in my bedroom and he barged in demanding to know what I had taken. He wanted it back NOW.

"I didn't take anything, what are you talking about?"

He was so agitated and angry. I don't know that I'd ever seen him like this before. I was scared. He was trying to push into my space.

I was very clear. "YOU ARE NOT WELCOME HERE, GET OUT!"

He stood at the door huffing, and trying to intimidate me further. He wanted me to admit something—that I'd taken something from him and was going through his stuff. I refused to engage. He was yelling now. He kept

going on and on. "How dare you go through my things!"

At this point I started to get scared. I knew I shouldn't be going through his things, but I also didn't know what was really behind that mask of his anymore. *What the fuck was this man hiding from me? Why was he so enraged?* His whole line of thinking gave me shivers up and down my whole body. I wasn't sure I really wanted to know the answers to those questions.

The next day while I was at work, Charlie bought a safe and put everything he could from his room inside. He was going to make damn sure I never touched his stuff again. Paranoid, indeed.

All summer Charlie had been dealing with a kidney stone issue, and with all the stress from the case adding to everything, it was getting worse. It was starting to look like he was going to need surgery to break up the stone and he was in more and more pain. As the day before the hearing finally arrived, we got notice that he was trying to postpone the hearing citing the kidney stone issue. I was PISSED.

My lawyer had recommended that for court, I start out with a very strong stance and ask for no overnights. It was way easier to add time if things were going well then to take it away. He felt that with the offense, we needed to come out strong, and we had a good case for it. I was worried about the impact on the boys, but had to trust that without a clear picture of what was going on, following my lawyer's advice made the most sense.

I had waited six weeks to get him out of my space. I was being forced to live with someone who was becoming more and more abusive towards me every day. My lawyer followed up with an emergency hearing request and the next morning, court was back on.

We walked into the hearing knowing that this was the first time I would have publicly spoken out against him. I had a speech written as to why my support for him

changed. I knew that it would be called into question and I would have to explain myself. Our motion laid out our points and asked that he be required to move and that he should not have any overnights with the children, but we offered lots of after school and weekend time. I didn't want the boys going back and forth between houses constantly either.

My lawyer thought that we had a good chance of getting it with the offense history, but that would depend on the judge. I would absolutely need to answer why my support for him had now changed. I was as calm and prepared as I could be.

The hearing started with the judge going over the motion we filed. We had all our paperwork done ahead of time—financials, everything. We stated he had a home to move into—and it was paid for in full—he just refused to move. The judge thought that was ridiculous, clearly, he needed to get out if I didn't want him there anymore. Winning!

And then the other side asked to share their perspective. They were going to try to counter my arguments. Charlie was compliant with probation and considered low risk in his treatment program. He needed witnesses to show up fast and speak for him or she was going to grant my motion to restrict overnights on the spot.

We both took the stand—going over what had been happening in the house. What I had been seeing. How bad things were and how unsafe I felt in my home. He took the stand and played the victim. I did all this to him. I dated openly in front of him. I cuckolded him in his own home. He went as far as to bring up me being intimate behind closed doors in my own home with Marcus. This was certainly something Charlie and I had done numerous times—so what was the issue here? He chose to stay in the house, knowing that I was dating. He

was trying to make a case that I was unfit, I was a drunk, I was unstable, and therefore the children were better off with him.

Everything he brought up was irrelevant. But what was relevant was that his probation officer and treatment therapist stood by him as a parent and supported him having the children unsupervised. Without a third party backing me—I was out of arguments. The court could not revoke overnights with what I had provided. The judge was clear—and I took her at her word. With what I had provided, it was not enough. I would have to find more data.

We settled that very intense two-hour hearing with 50/50 and in the rush of it all, ended with a schedule that had the boys going back and forth between houses four times a week. We would be next door from each other so I hoped it would help ease that transition, but it certainly felt like a lot.

That evening the boys were fighting. Charlie was trying to talk to me about what happened. He was blaming me again—I did this. I stole Christmas from him because the judge said they could wait until nine am to go over there, meaning early Christmas morning would be with me. Everything was still all my fault.

While we were arguing, Milo started screaming at the top of his lungs. Now this kid screams a LOT already, but this was different. Something was very wrong. We ran over to where they were—Ethan had been trying to get him out of his room and Milo was trying to get in. In all the fuss, Milo had gotten his hand caught in the doorjamb and Ethan was holding it shut as hard as he could.

Whelp, off to the emergency room we went. Remember when I talked about how connected Milo was to me? That kid certainly knows when I'm not OK. Charlie stayed with the other two boys while I took Milo

in. The ER didn't think his finger was broken, but the next day they called me back and radiology had disagreed. He had a compression fracture in his hand bones from being smashed in the door and he was going to need a cast.

Over the next couple of days, Charlie worked on moving out. He just needed enough things moved to be able to sleep there until he could get beds for the boys. The judge required him to move before his surgery which was scheduled for the day after Christmas. That only left him with three days to move.

Christmas was fairly uneventful that year. We had already set everything up at my house and after enough back and forth, I told him if he could stop being an asshole, we could do Christmas morning together since it was all set up here already. He calmed down and let the boys have their last two-parent Christmas together.

I had agreed to take Charlie to his surgery and pick him up. He wouldn't be able to drive himself and would likely have a week or two recovery. Everything went smooth enough—they thought they got most of the stone and hoped that he'd recover without complications. He recovered back at his house and the kids stayed the rest of Christmas break with me.

I took off work so that I could be home with my boys. It was the first time in over a year that my house was my own again. I spent that time pulling everything I could find of Charlie's out of it. I went through my entire kitchen removing all of the stuff that was his before we got together.

Something unique about me is my memory. I remember everything. Most of the time it is helpful, but sometimes it can be a curse. I remembered where every kitchen gadget or item came from, whether we got it together or had it prior, who wanted it and purchased it, and whether it was a gift from his family or mine. I piled

everything in one corner and made it as easy as I could to get his stuff out of my space for good.

He took offense to everything I did. How dare I think about things as his versus mine. I had been thinking that the whole time, he assumed. Me wanting to create my own space, was negating the marriage. I was trying to do what I could to move forward and to feel safe in my space again. He did not approve.

Once Charlie had healed enough from surgery we began the back and forth parenting plan ordered by the court. Four times a week the children would be now transitioning between homes.

The very first night the children spent over at Charlie's, the first time my house was child-free, the first time I was truly alone with my thoughts and my feelings was when everything I had been storing finally started to hit me.

I lay in my bed, tears streaming down my face. My family was broken. Being away from my children like this felt unnatural and wrong. I was scared, hurt, sad, betrayed, and completely alone. This was not what I wanted to happen. This was not how I wanted my life to look. I cried and cried that night. I knew it would get easier as time wore on, but in that moment everything really really sucked.

I still took the boys to school most days as it was on my way to work, only now sometimes they just walked over from Charlie's house. I was grateful for the chance to see them every day even if it was just for a car ride.

Charlie would usually walk over to my house with them. He wanted to see me and talk to me as much as he could. He still felt he could change my mind or something, which completely confused me since he was the one who filed for divorce. He started this whole freaking thing, and yet he was unwilling to let go. He would try to get into arguments and engage me in a

discussion about everything. I put up boundaries which only angered him. He left what he believed were helpful "gifts" at my doorstep or would try to be generous in some way that he thought I would like. I did not like any of it. He was completely overstepping every boundary I ever tried to set.

My relationship with the kids also was not improving. In fact, it had been getting worse. They started not listening to a single thing I said. It was like I went from being an outsider to living in a war zone. I was having to create new boundaries with them too and be 100% consistent or the whole ship would blow. It was exhausting to say the least.

I had an idea that perhaps we could use therapy to help us navigate a parenting plan. Working with my own therapist that I had gone back to seeing regularly, she thought it might be worth trying. The more we could agree to without the lawyers, usually, the better.

I called one of the original supervisors that we had used back when we had supervised visitation. Charlie liked her a fair amount and she was very thorough in her reports. She was more than happy to try and help us. We scheduled a meeting for the following week.

She came over to my house, and Charlie met us there. The boys were over at his house with his mom watching TV, so we could talk privately.

She started out by explaining the various things that one could consider when negotiating a parenting plan, things worth discussing up front and putting down in writing. She got to the section about when one parent starts dating again, what you might talk about—and Charlie pushed his chair, got up, and stormed out of the room.

We paused and waited. He came back into the room and was very emotionally charged. He was pacing and jerky in his movements. He was going on and on about

how horrible I was to him. How dare I date in front of him and the boys like that. Every interruption the therapist tried to get in there was ignored.

He continued just like he did with me, talking to himself in circles around and around. She would go back and forth between letting him speak and trying to course correct the conversation in order to bring him back to being able to listen. If he directed a comment or question directly at me, I would respond. I did not take on his version of the truth as accurate, but I also refused to play into the argument.

After nearly two hours of this, she eventually said she needed to leave. She wanted to see if Charlie would let her see the boys before she left, as it had been over a year since she'd seen them last.

He continued to try to talk to me, even while agreeing to take her to see them. After some time, she was able to coerce him out of my house and back over to his.

She came back to say goodbye to me, and I told her that was how it had been since I decided I couldn't be with him anymore. I didn't know how to negotiate anything with him.

She said she tried really hard to get him to come back to reality but he just couldn't. Once he fixated on me, he could not stop. She was scared for me, and knew she couldn't leave him alone with me in the house, which is why she asked to see the boys, so he would have to leave with her.

She then told me she didn't think the living next door situation was going to work out. She felt that the level of obsession he had with me would only escalate and it would not surprise her if he began peeping in through my windows watching me. The thought creeped me out, but part of me also knew she was right. I thanked her for trying to help and she left.

The next step in the divorce process was to go to mediation. It's a required step to at least try mediation before you litigate in court. After the attempt with the therapist, my lawyer was pretty sure that we were not going to succeed at getting parenting time settled, but he thought we might at least settle assets. I was willing to try, but I wasn't even sure that was going to happen. Colorado is a very 50/50 state in all regards, but Charlie was appalled that I was fighting for custody and still expecting 50% of the assets. Yes, I didn't work for a good portion of our marriage, but I was absolutely an equal contributor to the household under the eyes of the court. Child custody had nothing to do with money.

My lawyer was also trying to get me to consider what third party we could hire to do a thorough look at my case and make a recommendation to the court in my favor. He still felt we had a good chance at making our case in the final hearing but only if we poured some money into specialists. I was totally blocked on how to proceed. Nothing felt right. Nothing felt like it was in integrity to what needed to happen. The truth was I had no idea what needed to happen. Indecision was pouring out of me everywhere. I was still so angry at Charlie for filing for divorce and going this far with it all. He went as far as to try to throw the divorce out, but I would have to agree to do so. Well, that wasn't happening, but I wasn't even sure why I was then punishing him for filing. Was it just because he had the guts to do it first?

Mediation day came. I was pretty calm as I knew I wouldn't have to do this face-to-face with Charlie. The mediator goes back and forth and tries to get each side to agree to the other's demand to keep it all out of court. It's a very aggressive process and you never know what the other side actually said.

We wanted to start with money, hoping that Charlie wouldn't push, and we could get through that first. But

nope—he wanted to start with custody. Well, truthfully, he wanted to start with throwing the whole thing out, but that wasn't going to happen. Again, I was confused. *He fucking filed, why is he playing games now?* The court system isn't about scaring me to come running back. He truly seemed to feel like it was—and he just thought I was too stubborn to go back now. It only infuriated me further.

So OK fine, we'll start with custody. He wanted 50/50 custody, period. Well, I didn't like that. The mediator pushed, what would I agree to? 40/60? 30/70? I made something up—two days a week, he could have that. The mediator went back. Nope, he'll only agree to 50/50. Well, that wasn't happening. It was already impossible with the schedule we had. Plus, all the kid's activities—I still had to take them. He had been expecting me to pick them up, take them, and drop them back off with him. I wasn't their chauffeur or their babysitter—I was their mother. It was all insanity.

So, if I wasn't going to agree to 50/50 and he wasn't budging, where did that leave us? The mediator called out my indecision. He saw how unsure I was about everything and told me that's exactly what Charlie was responding to. Who fucking cared if he filed first? The fact that I was upset about it only implied I didn't want to end the marriage. Well, that didn't feel good to hear, but I guess on some level the idea of the safety of the whole family unit being gone did really scare me. I had to get really clear about what I actually wanted here or we would continue to go nowhere.

The other option on the table was asking for a Parental Rights Evaluator to get involved, citing the offense and the unknown nature of his mental health. I sat on that for another round of back and forth and finally agreed that was the next step. We were done negotiating custody.

Now, that still left finances which was what we actually wanted to accomplish. Of course, Charlie did not like that we bailed on negotiating custody, so he was going to play hard ball here. He claimed that there was a case for a contribution argument in that he contributed a larger amount to the marriage than I did. He wanted to keep our entire investment account. *What the ever-loving fuck?* We spent nearly 100 thousand dollars on his criminal defense, not to mention he was still not working, and I had been for the last year.

We went back and forth and back and forth. I wanted to split down the middle. He eventually came back with an offer that was essentially 45/55. It would be more expensive to fight this out in court than it would be to take it, and it would mean that I no longer had to report expenses to him or get his permission for financial decisions. We took it. After seven hours of mediation, we had one half accomplished, and a plan forward for custody. Someone else could help sort all this out. It was too muddy for me. I couldn't see clearly. I only knew that my gut was saying 50/50 was wrong. I was angry, scared and hurt, but some part of me also knew something else was at play here and I had to listen to that feeling and not settle.

That night the boys were scheduled with Charlie. I got home and he messaged me to let me know that Ethan had an earache. Ethan hasn't had an ear infection since he was a baby. No coincidence that another legal fight between us and another kid wasn't feeling well. I brought over some garlic oil to put in Ethan's ear to help soothe the pain. It was the natural remedy I'd used since he was a baby and it always worked. I gave him a hug in his bed and left. I was not comfortable in Charlie's house at all. Again, Charlie wanted to talk to me. He was frustrated I wouldn't negotiate custody. He wanted to know what I wanted. I told him I really didn't know. I had no idea how

to put this together; nothing felt right. He tried to keep me talking and I walked away.

He screamed at me, "Fine just walk away like you always do." The victim in him was so strong.

That was the last time I was ever in his house.

Chapter 13

I had a work trip scheduled for May of 2019, which was less than a month away. I was supposed to be going to Europe to help our office move locations. My role as IT Manager included being the project manager for our large Enterprise Resource Planning (ERP) migration and office location move on top of keeping up with my team. Going was the final step in a six-month long project and it was really important that I be there in person to complete it. My mom had offered to fly in from Hawaii and take my place on my parenting time.

My mom's plan was to fly out and stay with me for three weeks. I would be gone for 12 days, and she could take my parenting time in my place. I was not comfortable leaving the boys with Charlie any longer than I had to.

Before I left, I met with our newly assigned Parental Rights Evaluator. She was a retired mental health and family therapist and had many credentials and years of experience helping families sort out what needed to happen in difficult situations. I was hopeful that she could help me see through this mess and come up with a cohesive solution.

We met for over an hour and I brought her all of the documentation that I had been keeping on every transition, every fight, and every outburst that had occurred since the temporary orders hearing. At my lawyer's suggestion I took extensive notes. I explained my fears, my uncertainties, all of it. She asked if I felt a full psychological evaluation was in order, and I said I thought it was. We needed to know what we were dealing with here. She agreed and said that would mean I would have to have one too—there is no double standard. That

was fine with me too, I was not concerned about me in that regard. Overall, I left that meeting with hope that this was finally going to start to come together.

I went to Europe and had a very successful project finale. It was weird for me to be gone from the boys that long as I had never been away from any of them for more than a couple of days. Every time they were with my mom, they would FaceTime me. If they were with Charlie, they would not. Charlie even messaged that Axel was missing me, and I told him I was available to talk to him, but there was no call. None of that surprised me and I was so grateful that at least my mom was there to make sure that they stayed connected.

I got home on a Thursday evening. The boys technically weren't due back to me until Saturday, but because things were how they were there was not much I could do about seeing them sooner. When I finally did see them, they fell into my lap and Axel cried and Milo wouldn't leave my side for nearly an hour. Axel said he wished that Friday was a Mommy day because he really wanted to come see me yesterday, but he couldn't. I hugged him and shared that I missed him, too, and was so glad to be home.

The kids were so confused. They understood the concept of Mommy days and Daddy days, but they did not understand why things were so different at both houses and why we were no longer together.

One morning Milo woke up and the first thing out of his mouth was, "Why are you mad at Daddy? You shouldn't be mad at Daddy anymore!" I asked what he meant and why he thought that. He told me, "Daddy told us."

That evening Ethan said, "You should forgive Daddy so we can be all together again." I understood then. They had clearly been told that me being mad at Daddy was the reason that the family was not together. Again, this

was all my fault. I did my best to redirect and explain that while I was upset with Daddy, that was not the reason we could not be together. That concept is pretty hard for young kids to understand.

The alienation attempts continued. The children started saying Daddy wanted them to go over to his house, because he was lonely and missed them when they were gone. He was putting the weight of so much on their shoulders. I documented all of it, and funneled it to the evaluator.

Earlier that year I had asked Charlie about enrolling the boys in summer camp and whether he would need childcare for his days too as I looked for programs to sign them up for. He said yes and agreed that a full-time program made the most sense. When the time came to start their summer program he waited until after they had started to try to get permission from probation to pick them up. The program coordinator called me asking for permission to release them to walk unsupervised across the busy recreation center parking lot to meet him—without any prior practice or conversation or guidance. I was adamantly opposed to that and refused. I would be happy to pick them up, it was not a problem. He didn't like that either, so instead he decided they just wouldn't go on his days. If I had them that day, they came to my house and I took them to camp and picked them up. If not, then they went to his house.

While it seemed like an OK solution, camp had already been paid for in full and it meant the boys missed out on the pool days, and other field trips that were scheduled. It also added another set of transitions and confusion in the mornings. Axel would tell me that he didn't like waking up at Daddy's house, just to come to my house early, so he could be taken to camp. Axel would ask me if he could go to camp on water play day, but when I said we would have to check with Daddy, he

immediately changed his mind not wanting to ask Charlie.

More physical signs of distress were showing up. In camp one day Axel was sitting with his friend and peed on himself. He was now six and had been potty trained for four years. This was not normal for him at all. Divorce is hard on kids, but this was getting crazy. Every effort I made to reduce transitions and stress on the boys was met with defensiveness that I was taking away from his parenting time. He could not see the impact that his actions were having on them. All he could see was what he wanted and felt he deserved.

The evaluation was due in August right before our next court date. Days before it was filed, we had the worst transition between households to date. The boys came over with Charlie on Saturday as normal. They had been playing video games all day and didn't want to stop. They kept saying no they wanted to stay with him and not come to my house at all. Then they began physically fighting me to go back to his house. Screaming and wailing, hitting me, everything. Axel and Ethan both ran back to Charlie's house and hid from him multiple times. Charlie went back to get them over and over. Even Milo was aggressive and hitting me, and pushing me away.

The aggression went on for over an hour before I finally got them in the door and into their rooms and things began to calm down. I had no idea what had happened, but I certainly knew who had caused this. I sent the evaluator a message telling her what had happened and asking for advice. Things could not go on like this any more.

I had figured out by now that the next-door living situation wasn't going to work. After the failed attempt to mediate I had even begun house shopping and was in the process of buying another home, hopeful that I would be moving soon.

Charlie had just continued showing up to my house whenever he wanted and it was more and more uncomfortable. I caught him on more than one occasion walking up and down the street in front of my house trying to look in. I set up cameras to feel some sort of safety that I would at least know if he was ever there. I could not have any friends over, and could not even think about trying to date. I was being watched. It was really doing a number on my nervous system.

The evaluator's report came out the following week. It was 82 pages long and detailed so much of what had been going on. The psych reports had some serious diagnoses for Charlie. Major depression and anxiety and a personality disorder diagnosis. He now officially had dependent personality disorder. The more I read about it, the more it made so much sense; he had been hyper dependent and even obsessive with me, and that was now shifting to dependency on the children to meet his emotional needs. My report came through as psychologically normal. The primary suggestion for me was giving more thought about how dating might also impact the kids and something I would need to consider more in the future. I did not disagree with this assessment at all.

I also learned that Charlie had recorded and transcribed the big awful transition we had, and sent it over to the evaluator. He thought he was in the right and was showing off at how much the boys didn't like me anymore. I got to read the sides of the conversation that I didn't hear before where he was encouraging their behavior and telling them over 20 different times how much he loved and missed them and how cute they were being and it just went on and on. It was insane! The evaluator beautifully called him out on the damage he was causing.

With all that data, the report was very good for me. However, the final recommendation was really the part that mattered. The recommendation was that we would essentially keep 50/50 time, but some of the decision making would be solely on me. Mental health decisions, education decisions, and extracurricular decisions would not be joint. There were allowances for his restrictions where I would take them and depending on when the next transition was, I would keep them. She really tried to think of everything.

While it was not what I wanted or even expected, I understood her viewpoint and really appreciated how she put the pieces together. It was very comprehensive. It felt like it was worth a try at least to see how it went, and so we drafted a settlement. We wrote up a nearly identical agreement to her recommendation and sent it over to Charlie's lawyer. All that was left to do now was to wait and see.

Chapter 14

Our settlement offer was ignored for over a month. He didn't respond by the deadline the court gave us to finalize it. My lawyer and I were confused again. Did he still think I was going to drop the case? What was going on?

I had also now begun the process of moving. I was under contract for a new house across town that I really loved and was simultaneously finalizing the details of putting my current home on the market to sell. I was so grateful that we did settle the financials already, so I didn't have to wait to get into a safer space.

While financials were settled in technicality, the actual division of assets had not yet happened. The accounts in my name, I dispersed immediately. The joint investment account however, was not something I could disperse by myself. I also could not remove his name from my home's title without his notarized signature.

In order to buy a new home, I needed more down payment money. In order to sell my home I needed him off the title. I messaged Charlie that it had been past the 30-day deadline in the order and I needed him to complete his portion. I was ignored as usual.

My lawyer got involved, and we were promised by his attorney that the money would be divided and that he would agree to whatever I needed to sell the home.

Again, nothing happened. My realtor got involved and offered suggestions to help. He refused to take his name off the title because he was still on the mortgage. Refinancing a mortgage when I was just going to sell it made no sense.

The other option was to have him involved in the sale process. I did not like that option either. There is a

ton of back and forth and negotiating and contracts involved with selling a home. He would have no legal say, but would have to stay cooperative.

Finally the title office came up with a solution. They would allow me to sell the home, even though technically the title was not in my name, as long as he agreed to sign it over to me as part of the sale process to the new owners. It was convoluted but it seemed to satisfy Charlie's needs.

Getting the investments dispersed took just as much back and forth. He had to speak to the advisors and sign off on the division, and then when I called, there'd be another step that would take another week or two to get him to handle.

It seemed like everything was impossible for him to do. At the time it also felt incredibly intentional as a way to punish me for moving further away.

The stalking efforts had become more and more obvious too. Marcus had stayed over to help me reinstall new bedroom doors on the boy's rooms as they had destroyed the other ones. Charlie was always there watching, sitting on his driveway every time we came and went with tools and supplies.

Finally, with less than a day left until the closing on my home, everything was completed. I had access to the cash I needed, and there were no more delays.

The new house I purchased had four bedrooms, instead of three, so the boys could each have their own room. It was set up in a way that the kids' rooms were all upstairs, and the master was downstairs, so when I didn't have them it wouldn't feel quite as lonely in my house. I was really excited to have a house that was 100% my own.

We then had yet another difficult transition. By comparison it was nothing, but the same element of Charlie encouraging them not to be with me by saying things like, "Aww, I really miss you when you're gone,

too." The energy behind it was exactly the same as before. Thankfully, by moving across town there was no opportunity for them to run between houses anymore. I merely had to get them in the car, and drive away.

I was trying to find ways to reconnect with my children and so when Axel had a school presentation on a Friday, I decided to go and see him. Normally Friday was a Charlie pickup day, but since he couldn't visit the school, and I was able to take off, I wanted to make sure to go and show support for him. He was so happy to see me as he didn't think I would've been able to get off work. He was so excited, he wanted to know if he could come home with me, even though it wasn't my day.

We called Charlie and asked, and to my surprise he agreed. Ethan didn't want to leave with us, so it was just going to be Axel and me, which he was THRILLED about. He wanted to go get ice cream, and play games, and watch a movie—just me and him. When we sat down to watch a movie, he climbed in my lap. But then he started trying to kiss me on the lips and became aggressive and affectionate. It made me extremely uncomfortable. I asked him to stop, not wanting to jar him, but knowing that this was not good. What the hell was going on with my kid?

The word grooming had begun to linger in my mind. I talked to my lawyer and therapist and mom about my concerns.

Grooming is defined in the Oxford Dictionary as "the action by a pedophile of preparing a child for a meeting, especially via an internet chat room, with the intention of committing a sexual offense."

I was trying very hard not to jump to conclusions here but all of the behavior changes had me incredibly uncomfortable. I knew that grooming was not something that happened quickly, it took time to desensitize the victims. And very often it was easiest to desensitize

victims that you already had access to and had a familial and trusting relationship with.

My drive to go get my children, and run away with them was so strong. All I wanted to do was get as far away from this as possible. But the rational part of me knew that doing so would only make things a whole lot worse.

To take care of myself and my mental health on top of therapy and daily runs, Marcus and I would also go mountain bike riding most weekends. It was a fun adventure we could do together that meant we could spend time together as friends and help me take my mind off what was happening in the rest of my world.

Eventually, we even began sleeping together again, although we had to keep it completely private, as I was now his direct supervisor. It was a line I had not wanted to cross, but once everything with Charlie escalated the way they did, spending time with Marcus felt like my only safe place to be.

This time I was extra careful to not have him around the children. I truly did not want to cause them any more confusion or give Charlie any more ammunition to use against me.

Most Fridays after work, I'd go to his house and he'd cook me dinner, and we'd watch a movie or play video games. Saturday we'd go for a mountain bike ride before I had to get the boys. Spending time with Marcus was easy, fun, and truly helped keep me sane.

That fall we were riding down one of my favorite trails, as you get closer to the bottom you go through these fields of beautiful yellow flowers. Downhill riding was my favorite, and this particular trail was perfect for it. As I rode through the field, I very clearly heard a message, in a voice that wasn't my own, "Everything is going to work out. You are all going to be OK." And in that moment, I knew that somehow, someway, it would be.

It had now been over a month of waiting for the settlement, and with more and more weird things going on, my lawyers and I agreed it was time to pull the offer. This meant making the decision that we were going to court. We felt we were more than fair and followed the recommendations to a T. The only thing we could assume now was that Charlie's mental health was also further deteriorating, which was in itself a huge concern for us. We also needed the evaluator to update the report, because clearly there was more going on that we could see. We still hoped we were wrong, but I began to feel something really dark was happening in that house.

As soon as we pulled the settlement, the bottom dropped out from my world once again. I was driving the boys to school on a Tuesday morning. I remember that day clearly, as I also had a big presentation I was working on to give in front of the whole company at work. I was going over it in my head as I was driving, and had totally tuned out whatever the boys were talking about. I pulled into the school parking lot and Axel said to me excitedly, "Sometimes I suck on Daddy's fingers!"

WHAT?!! I didn't say a word. I didn't know what to say. *What the ever-loving fuck is going on?* I sent them off to school and went to work. I did not know how to handle this. I had been more and more uncomfortable with what was coming up—but this? The realization hit me like a ton of bricks. My kids were indeed being fucking groomed by their father. The same father that I supported through a criminal proceeding. Then of course I was reminded that this was the criminal proceeding where he showed up to meet an 11 and 14-year-old for sex. *Fuck fuck fuck!* I finally started to see it! That meetup was no accident. He was not "helping them." He always intended to go through with it. *What on earth could I do about this now?*

I flashed back to all the things that happened before. The hard drives he had me put in the trash. The sexual favors he wanted me to preform with other men.

No raid was ever done on our house. No one ever searched his devices. I knew he had kept nude photos of me as a teenager even, justifying that I was his wife now.

No one ever questioned me or the children. I was in such a state of shock back then I couldn't even process anything beyond putting one foot in front of the other. It had never occurred to me then that my husband was anything other than a good man, a good husband, and a good father.

What the fuck was I going to do now?

I asked my lawyers first what to do. I was well aware that in the middle of a custody dispute adding allegations to one side never looks good. I would need to be incredibly strategic with how I went about this. They suggested talking to the boys' therapist first. Good—I was the primary person taking them to that appointment since sessions had been falling on my days.

The following week I spoke to their therapist before Axel's appointment. I told her what Axel had said in the car and that I was concerned but I wasn't sure if I needed to be crazy concerned or what. It was such an odd thing for him to say. She suggested that if it comes up again, I should respond and ask him to show me what he means.

At the same time the Parental Rights Evaluator was starting on her report update. I met with her and gave her the update and what I was worried about. I was not going to jump to conclusions, but if there was ANY validity to what was going on, then I absolutely wanted him to have no more than supervised visitation time. She understood and also agreed with the therapist that asking him to show me was the right thing to do if it came up again. Otherwise, she listened to my concerns about his mental health, that he continued not to follow her

recommendations, and that there was more going on here.

A couple more weeks went by and it came up again. I was putting Axel to bed in his room and asked about the finger sucking he mentioned with Daddy. He giggled nervously and hid under the covers, clearly very uncomfortable. I asked him to show me and he stuck his thumb in and out of his mouth...exactly like I had feared he would. I let it go, but the conversation was recorded on my phone. I knew that I was going to need more clear evidence this time.

I called the therapist back the next day and shared with her what happened. She told me that if Axel had done that in front of her, she'd be obligated to report it to Child Protective Services. With that statement, my lawyers agreed that despite the custody battle, it was time to get the authorities involved. I called CPS and made the report. I also emailed probation and the sex offender therapist with what I had learned. I was not going to let this one get swept under the rug.

I dropped the boys off at the school the next day with no clue what was going to happen next. It was a Charlie pickup day, and I just had to wait. I didn't hear anything all day or night. I was NOT sleeping well at that point, just wracking my brain on what could be going on. I knew the systems were slow, but sheesh.

The following day was my day to pick the boys up. I was relieved that I'd have them back at least to make sure they were OK. I also got a call from the CPS case worker that day. He wanted to meet with Axel and interview him. He asked if he could come to the house and meet him here. I agreed, as I was already picking him up and so we could meet him right after school. I picked up Axel early from school. He was surprised but happy to see me. He really liked special Mommy time. On the way to my house, he told me that they didn't see Daddy yesterday.

Grandma had picked them up from school and stayed at Daddy's house and they couldn't even call Daddy. He said Grandma wouldn't tell them what was going on and he was very scared. I told him that I didn't know what was going on either, but I would message Grandma and try to find out.

When we got to my house the case worker was just behind us. I told Axel he was kind of like a therapist so he could talk to him. It was a word he understood already, and I didn't want to scare him. The case worker talked to him a little to try to get him to relax, but Axel was so uncomfortable he was hiding under the kitchen table. Then the guy asked him point blank if he still sucked on Daddy's fingers, because Mommy had told him about that. Axel just kept hiding under the table and had a really hard time speaking. I was honestly shocked that he asked him that outright and had no idea how to help the situation. Eventually Axel says very quietly they don't do that anymore.

"OK good," the case worker said. He packed up and got ready to leave. I spoke to him about all of Charlie's past and my concerns. He just said he'd reach out to Charlie and would get back to me.

Well, OK then. I was surprised. I thought this was a protection agency, no? It shocked me honestly that he pushed on a seven-year-old like that for information. No way Axel was going to open up to him like that, but there really wasn't more I could do so I just had to let it play out.

Charlie's mom also had never responded to me about what had happened the day before. All three boys were very upset the next morning. They knew it was normally time to go back to Daddy's again and they didn't know if they were even going to get to see him. Ethan told me Milo had been crying and screaming all night because he didn't want Grandma. I told them that if Daddy wasn't

with them, they could always ask Grandma to call me and I would be more than happy to pick them up and they could be home with me. That seemed to settle them.

I messaged Charlie and asked him what was going on. Was there a problem and did I need to take the boys? They were very upset and confused about the Grandma sleepover, and I did not understand why no one called me. He played dumb and said there was no problem and had no idea what I was even talking about. Of course not.

Charlie picked the boys up and had his two-and-a-half days with them as usual. Whatever interruption had happened seemed to have passed. I didn't hear back from CPS until another week or so. They told me that probation had polygraphed Charlie about the incident and cleared him. My report to probation had meant that he lost access to the boys for 48 hours and that's why Grandma was there. But NO ONE CALLED ME. I was so frustrated. When I tried to get the details from probation, about what they specifically cleared him for, I was told I did not have permission to see his file and they couldn't tell me anything. *Wait, what? This guy has full access to my kids, and you can't let me see his fucking file?*

Yeah, I was angry. And frustrated. And felt stuck. The system was so broken. But what could I do about that now? What I needed to do was get my kids out of there as unharmed as I possibly could.

I was still in therapy. I was going through so much chaos it helped to be able to sort through. My therapist was also shocked by what was going on and that no one seemed to care.

I was no longer willing to negotiate parenting time. I didn't want Charlie ever having unsupervised access to them. This was ALL not OK. And he didn't even seem to know that it wasn't OK. I wasn't sure which was worse.

What I also finally began realizing was that I still had some part of me running some idea that there could be

some sort of a family again. I was angry that he filed for divorce. We bought the house right fucking next door. I told my lawyer and the evaluator that they should tell me what we should do. I even considered dropping the damn divorce when things got messy. It felt like I'd have more rights to my kids if we just stayed married. Which was only sort of true. I didn't ever actually DECIDE what I wanted. I knew I was upset and angry and scared, but some part of me still wanted my family to be able to stay together.

If I'm willing to get real honest with myself, some part of me even missed the marriage. There's comfort and partnership and friendship that had until very recently remained there. In the deepest part of me, I did hope that someday things might be different. He would get real help, and heal his deviances. Perhaps there was another chance for us if that could happen. I knew it was unlikely and really not healthy to think like that. On the other end, I also felt very ashamed of ever considering the possibility, and would not even admit as much to myself.

I truly hated the kids going back and forth like they had been. I could see the stress it was causing them. Their behavior was all over the place. I was exhausted. They were exhausted. We spent so little actual quality time together. I missed my family.

I was living in indecision. I didn't want to be married to a sex offender, but I did want my family. I had no idea how to reconcile that and so instead I gave all that decision-making power to everyone else. It was someone else's job to figure out how to put this together in a way that protected me and my kids. My lawyer, the therapist, the evaluator. I had all these people around me, advising me. But all of them together meant I never had actually had to make a real decision. I didn't ever say no this is what needs to happen and why. I just gladly let them take

over and tell me what was best for my family.

And, I realized, if I wasn't careful it was going to also be CPS, and then the judge, deciding what was going to happen long-term. I could see the timeline playing out so clearly. CPS was clearly useless, and borderline harmful. Axel telling me he was sucking on his dad's fingers wasn't enough for them. It terrified me to think of what would be enough.

I also remembered clearly what the judge said in the temporary orders hearing. She would need more than my word and my fears to budge from 50/50.

My mom's words kept repeating in my head to me over and over, "How bad does it have to get?"

The boys were signed up for skiing lessons that year. This would be the first year they had ever done them. Charlie and I talked about it back in September. He agreed I could sign them up and at the time I assumed we'd be settled by then and swapping every other weekend, so I didn't focus on the specific day it was scheduled for. They were scheduled to go up Saturday mornings, now still a Charlie day. They transferred back to me at 5:30pm Saturdays. So, this event cut into his main weekend time.

I sent him an email asking him to meet me at the parking lot with the boys so I could take them to ski class the week before it started. The ski lessons were 40 or so minutes away and would have lots of kids around. I just assumed I'd have to take them due to the restrictions. I had bought the lessons and all their gear as well. I had also bought myself a ski pass that year and was intending to go up and learn to ski myself while they were in class.

Charlie responded and wanted to negotiate the schedule with me. Bear in mind, we knew then that we'd be in court at the end of February for our final orders hearing. It was early January. The schedule was about to be changed again one way or another. The children's

therapist had been super clear that the hardest thing for kids is to keep having the schedule change. They need to be able to count on where they're going to be and when. An activity was different because it was logical, but a total change of days would throw them off again.

I was not willing to negotiate a complete schedule change for an activity that he agreed they could do—especially eight weeks before we were about to go to court. It was nuts. He wanted to get a day back and I was not budging. This was about them and what was best, and classes were only seven weeks and then it would go back to what it was or be whatever the court then decided. I told him to meet me in the parking lot with the boys at 7:30 am so we could get up there in time.

That morning he showed up like I asked, but he wouldn't let the boys out of the car. He started texting me again wanting to negotiate. He was literally holding the boys hostage in the car while trying to get me to agree to a change. It was blackmail. I was pissed, but I was again standing my ground. This was not going to fly. We sat in that parking lot for 40 fucking minutes arguing over text, when the boys needed to be up on the mountain for their first class.

The more frustrated I became, the more volatile he got. When I told him it felt like he was holding the children hostage, he freaked out and threatened to leave. I finally agreed to discuss the schedule with the therapist and evaluator and would agree to what was best for them to get him to let them out of the car. This was literally the 10th time of me pleading with him to just let them out of the damn car—he finally did.

We went up the mountain and I got them to class just barely on time. Milo was incredibly clingy and shy with his teachers. He wanted me to stay close and would not leave to go with his class. I sat there as long as I could and eventually left him there, hoping he would calm down

and enjoy the class. While I waited for them to be finished, I messaged the evaluator about what had just happened. *What the fuck was he thinking? This was nuts.*

When I picked up the boys, Milo hadn't skied at all. He had refused to even try. His emotions and panic about leaving me meant he couldn't enjoy class. Next week, I hoped would be better. Ethan and Axel had a good time. I learned that their instructor was a minor, which was only another reason Charlie couldn't come up here.

We left and went back to my house. We got back home around two and Milo desperately needed a nap. Charlie had tried to say that I should bring them back to him for the three-and-a-half hours and I told him no. That was so unfair to them. This was the sort of crap that he constantly pulled. Because it was HIS time, HE deserved it to be equal no matter what the cost to the kids. It was always about him, never about them.

We continued to fight about their ski lessons all week. The evaluator tried to help, and he started not responding to her until the last minute. The classes had been expensive, and it was so unfair to make the boys go through this when he had already agreed they could go. Eventually Charlie said that he had permission to take them from probation and so he wanted to be the one to take them up there if I wasn't going to negotiate. Why didn't he lead with that? I told them all that their instructor was a minor and either he didn't believe me or didn't care. I was so freaking frustrated.

I met them in the next class to hand over skis and equipment. I also had all my stuff with me and decided that him taking them to class didn't have to stop me from going up as well and learning just like I planned. If he wanted to drive up too, well that was his prerogative. I tried to avoid seeing them, again not wanting to cause problems of any kind, but the boys spotted me. They wanted to ski with me during class. I was learning to ski

myself, and so I was going on beginner lifts, and sometimes we'd ride up together. I wanted them to stay with their instructor and learn, but saying hi was fine. I disappeared before class was over, so I didn't have to run into Charlie again.

The conflict continued and was such a cause of stress and frustration for everyone. I talked to the evaluator about it extensively. She agreed with me that he was only trying to demand HIS time, and that he could not see any of the impact of what was going on with the boys. He was also pissed that I showed up on the mountain and interacted with the boys on HIS parenting time.

Another therapist friend of mine suggested that the conflict had gotten to the level of totally ridiculous that I should visualize a cartoon character whenever interacting with him. There's this idea that if we can bring some comic relief, we can ease the immediate panic to the situation. Things had really reached that level and so I went as far to rename him on my phone to "Pedo." It was something, anything, I could do to take some power away from him and the situation.

On another ski lesson morning I accidentally had forgotten Milo's ski boots in my rush to meet them to get them their equipment. When I realized it, I knew there wasn't anything to do but run back to my house to get them while they waited.

But Charlie wanted to follow me to my house. He thought it would be faster, although my house was in the opposite direction of the ski hill. I started to panic.

"Absolutely not! You can come to the end of the neighborhood, but no further."

I was trying to be accommodating, but having him anywhere near my new home sent me into a complete panic spiral.

Charlie looked over at Axel and said, "Mommy is going to make us late because she won't let Daddy come

to her house." *OH, no he didn't!* There was the alienation right there! I responded, "You absolutely are NOT coming to my home—you have been stalking me!"

"Stalking you?" Now it was his turn to be mad. "Who was the therapist you took Axel to see without my permission?" I ignored him. I got into my car and headed back to my house for the boots. As I was driving away shaking I could hear him scream at me from the parking lot. "FUCK YOU, AMANDA! FUCK YOU!" All right in front of the kids.

I knew that accusing him of stalking in front of the boys was also not OK. I was kicking myself for losing my cool. But the idea of him coming to my home, for any reason whatsoever, had sent me into a full on panic attack. I had cameras up, but there was a reason I had been meeting him at the grocery store parking lot for any transition to my house. I didn't want him to know exactly where I was living. I could not handle the idea of him scoping out my new place and watching me.

I quickly drove back home, grabbed the boots, and drove back. I emptied the rest of the gear from my car right onto the parking lot and took off. I did not need any further interaction with Charlie. I knew the escalation between us was really harmful for the boys.

Axel continued to go to therapy regularly. He had now begun hearing voices in his head at night. He talked to both Charlie and I about it and we brought it up with the therapist. The voices were saying bad things about him, calling him bad names and insulting him. He tried to tell them to stop, and when he did, they just got louder. His therapist felt that he was doing some negative self-talk related to all the stress. She worked with him to name the voices and quiet them. It didn't help.

Another thing that came up in therapy was Axel was playing with a doll and then he decided to take a chopstick to the doll's crotch and smash it in over and

over. The therapist thought that was really a really odd thing for him to do—and something he'd never done before. She didn't feel it warranted reporting but definitely agreed something bigger was going on with him.

I could clearly see what was going on. Axel was the most emotionally and energetically sensitive of all the boys. He was very empathetic and as the middle child, he also really loved receiving special attention apart from his brothers. He was the perfect target for a predator. He didn't like when anyone got in trouble, and he especially wouldn't have wanted his Daddy in more trouble than he already was.

My resolve to help my kids through this only strengthened. There was no question anymore what was going on. My children were being groomed by their father for his own pleasure and it was completely disgusting.

My inability to choose a path had meant that we were now in this mess and it was my job to get us out of it.

My kids needed me to stand up and fight for them.

And dammit that's what I was going to do.

Chapter 15

My therapist was working with me extensively to get through this. I was exhibiting signs of PTSD and she wanted to try EMDR with me to help me calm my nervous system down, and help me not react so strongly to the constant battling going on. Every text message or phone call sent my nervous system into overdrive.

If my phone rang when I was out on a trail bike riding with Marcus, I would have an immediate panic moment that it could be Charlie—or worse, something else had happened and I was getting a call that the boys had been taken by social services. I had so many threads of possibilities swirling in my head causing it to be difficult to operate normally.

As the conflict progressed, so did my anxiety, and my therapist continued to try to offer me additional support. She also worked in the family court system sometimes, and understood the intricacies. She had read all the evaluator's reports and agreed with my assessment that there were some really dark things going on in that house.

One day as I was leaving her office, she stopped me and asked if I'd ever thought about talking to a psychic about what was going on. I was shocked to say the least to hear this from a traditional mental health professional, but I considered her question. Growing up my mom was very spiritual, and I always had some sense that more than the physical world was out there, but I steered clear from spirituality most of my adult life. But truthfully, at this point I was desperate. I mean, what could it hurt? I asked if she knew any good ones, but I was unsure if that even was a thing. She said she did and gave me a number.

I talked to a few of my more open coworkers about what my therapist said and they all agreed it couldn't hurt, and that I should go try.

My office also had a massage therapist come to the office every Thursday to offer 30 minute massages to employees. I regularly went and would often share some about what was going on with me. She too was going through a separation and we connected through our stories. Although her separation was not nearly as dangerous as mine was, there were similarities.

I told her about the suggestion to see a psychic and she said, "Oh, you need to see THIS lady." She knew the person that trained the person my therapist had recommended to me. She felt like I really needed to see a specific, very powerful woman. She normally had a months-long waiting list, but maybe if she knew the situation she would want to help. She figured I should at least try to see if I could get in. Again, what could it hurt, right?

I left that massage and googled her number on the walk back to my desk. As a surprise to me she immediately picked up the phone. I told her what was going on and that I needed help. She listened and told me she happened to have a cancellation open up and if I could come in next week, she could see me. *Well, OK then, I'll be there.*

Later I learned that you don't just get in to see this lady, like ever. Her waiting list is months and months long. She also never answers her phone in the middle of the day, but just so happened to have left it on while she was eating lunch that day. Sometimes she does get a cancellation and it's always for a specific person and a specific reason. This time it was for me.

I walked into her office the next week not knowing what to expect. I was desperate and totally open to whatever she had to say.

Her office was set up a lot like you'd expect. Crystals and deities everywhere. She had two rooms, one had her desk and phone, and the other was set up with just two chairs facing each other for readings.

She was finishing up a phone call when I entered. I just took a seat and waited. I removed my shoes and turned my phone to quiet and took off my watch. You could record the session, but you didn't want any interruptions.

She was a wonderfully feisty woman. That's the best way I can describe her. She was so sure of herself and had this way about her where she just told you how it was straight. No messing around. I love that in people and it usually takes someone so sure of themselves for me to listen to them over my own stubbornness.

She described her gift as though she saw angels and spirits as clear as other people in the room. They speak through her to bring messages to those who need to hear them. They were jumping up and down waiting to get started to talk to me. They were the ones who created this session for me to be here today.

She began by sharing a story that happened to me in a lifetime 500 years ago in the South of France. In that lifetime my husband at the time was an alcoholic. He was also physically violent and regularly beat me when he was drunk or didn't like something I did.

Things between us were mostly OK-ish until the children came. Then I would stand up to him more to protect the kids. I also stayed with him because of the children. I thought back then I couldn't make it on my own—as this was a time when women were still considered property themselves.

The similarities to thoughts that I had this time around was so eerie. She said things that were identical to what was currently running through my mind. Thoughts and fears that I never had shared with her. Then she told

me his name—Jean Charles. *Fucking hell.*

Then she said that in that lifetime there was a big fight between us and he ended up beating me to death. I was thrown down the stairs and never got up. She was watching this happen in front of her. As she was telling me this, the only thing I could think about was—well then what happened to the kids? After the scene finished, she said, "Your dying thought then was, 'Who is going to protect the kids now?'"

Sharing that still gives me shivers to this day.

In that lifetime, my sister took the children; he didn't want them. They were safe and were OK. But in this lifetime, I had a choice to make. I had to stand up once and for all and be DONE DONE with this. I had to decide that I was no longer going back or accepting anything from him ever again. I had to get a hold of the fear that my body remembered from being beaten and do what had to be done today. I had to finally let go of any lingering part of me that still believed reconciliation was possible.

I stood up in the room and said, "I'm done."

She said, "Say it like you really mean it."

I finally saw myself clearly in that moment. I saw how hard I had been holding onto the maybe things could resolve peacefully. Maybe he'd get better and we'd have the life we always wanted. In that instant I truly let go of ever reconciling or ever co-parenting with Charlie. It was time.

I shouted, "I'm SO FUCKING DONE!"

"Good. That's what they needed to hear. That's why your angels sat your ass down in that chair today. They've been dying to help you, but they needed you to finally choose."

Well, fuck. I'm choosing now.

I asked her to look into possible strategies for me—different options. She confirmed that Charlie was

incredibly deviant and pathological. He could lie and nothing about him had changed. His energy left a nasty taste in her mouth and she said he is someone she would cross the street to not have to walk past. The boys being around that energy was the cause of so much of what was going on with them, especially the voices in Axel's head.

She confirmed my deepest fears without me asking them. His soul was very wounded and abused. Lifetimes of repeated abuse created who he was today. I had seen the goodness in him at one point, and she was careful to check whether there was any part of him that was ready to face everything and begin to heal and change.

But no, he had no interest in healing. He was beyond stuck and only had been digging his hole deeper. Coming back from this was not something he was interested in.

She said I needed to leave no stone unturned. People will listen and I will have help. Ask everyone. Be respectful, but don't give up. There is more possible. She believed he had a ton of porn in his possession and if I could prove that the whole case would blow up on him as that was a major probation violation. I only hoped someone would actually listen to me.

I left that session a new person. She gave me the confidence to start to ask for help from more places. My energy shifted so dramatically; I was going to make this happen. I no longer had any doubt. I had help. I just had to follow the guidance.

There was only one outcome that I was going to let be possible here and everything I did from here on out, was just going to help make that happen.

I got to work later that day and walked into the office of some of my friends. I asked for their advice and help. Who else could I talk to? I got ideas. One woman had an uncle who worked for ICE. She had been following my story and decided she was fed up with the system too and wanted to reach out to him for help. Another called CPS from another county. I thought to ask my realtor, who

suggested I call the district attorney.

What started to unfold was nothing short of miraculous. The ICE connection put me in touch with Homeland Security. They were appalled that a felony sex offender had unsupervised access to my kids and that none of us were ever questioned back in 2016. They then put me in touch with the local federal agent who ended up being the same man that put the cuffs on Charlie in 2016. He listened to me and vowed to help me as best he could. He put me in touch with the detective in the local police department that could actually do something to help me, the same detective that stood next to the federal agent cuffing Charlie. These guys knew exactly who he was and both agreed to do anything they could to help me.

The local detective got CPS back involved to get Axel forensically interviewed about the finger sucking incident. However, since so much time had passed, Axel completely denied everything and that it ever happened. The detective didn't waver in his support. He knew that just because nothing was admitted, didn't mean that nothing happened. To him all it meant was that Axel didn't open up. His next steps were to try to get probation to let him into Charlie's devices.

Then I spoke to the district attorney. He listened to my story again and said he couldn't do much about it from his end, but he did have the original case file if it could be helpful. I had never seen it and so I said, "Yes, I would appreciate it if you would send it to me."

He had to do some work on it to redact some areas to release it to the public, but he could get it to me in a week or so. *OK, then!*

I pushed on CPS, I pushed on probation, going up the chain of command to the top. I emailed the head probation officer about the lack of enforcement of the probation restrictions in his department. I talked to

everyone I could think of for ideas, and then I followed through and I did everything I could think of and everything anyone else could think of too. I refused to hide from what happened, and instead used it to fuel my mission. I was not going to ever be left to question whether I did enough. If I didn't succeed, I knew I would only keep trying. There was no other option.

Not every avenue was fruitful, but I hoped that if I kept going enough of them would be. The DA's report took a couple of weeks, but when he sent it to me I immediately forwarded it to my lawyers. Criminal case files, once all identifying information is redacted, are 100% public record.

The case file he sent me was 241 pages long. It included reports from every single officer involved in the sting operation. There were multiple detailed reports from the perspectives of the officers charged with identifying men interested in the child sex trade.

I finally got the details that I never could get answers to before. I knew some of it, of course, but only from the perspective of Charlie who had clearly been minimizing everything.

I learned that day he had messaged a woman on an ad on Backpage. This website is no longer in existence, but it was the Craigslist for hookers. He was immediately offered two children, ages 11 and 14, and, after seeing photos and agreeing to the terms, he agreed to meet them that evening.

He drove to multiple locations to meet them at their request. First to a grocery store parking lot, and then to the hotel parking lot.

The most damaging part of all of it though was the text exchanges between him and the agent.

Charlie: "Hi "blossoms", this is Jim. Are there more than one of you? I'd love descriptions or pictures and rates please. Thanks!"

Agent: "Hi hun, got 2 girls they r kind of young" "got an 11 and 14 year old, the 14 year old is in the pic. 125hr 75 hh hun"

Charlie: "What does "kinda young" mean? Can you send pic or description? When can we meet?

Agent: "14 year old Mandy"

Charlie: "oh and rates?"

Agent: "!25 hh 75 hr or rates for both if ur interested"

Charlie: "I assume they're actually legal and just look young. That sounds illegal if it is more than a fantasy. Or a sting." "With that assumption in place—please confirm!—I'm very interested in doubles. When would work?"

Agent: "hun they are 11 and 14 years old, young but experienced. If its not your thing thats cool, not for everyone" "its 225 for both for h, 150 for both for hh. Got some times open this afternoon and later 2nite if u want to meet :)"

Charlie: "How would this work, where are you in all this? Are they sisters or something? Are you somewhere discreet?"

Agent: "sister, being as discrete as we can, looking for some nice guys. I dont play anymore, just my girls"

Charlie: "How do you know I'm not a cop—and how do I k now you aren't?" "On the flip side … How about 3. Or are you strict about not playing? Kidding, or creampie available?"

Agent: "wel im not a cop, and if u r then u have to tell me or its illegal"

Charlie: "I dont think cops really have to tell you. I'm not a cop, just nervous"

Agent: "I can record for u if u want, but I won't participate. Sry getting busy hun"

Charlie: "Recording would be good. Talk soon."

Agent: "baby thats fine. Thought I lost you.

Charlie: "didn't lose me."

Agent: "so you going to be in Durango ready to go at 9 right. Cuz I gotta schedule to keep ok baby"

Charlie: "so where are you at?"

Agent: "hi hun, go to the Albertsons parking lot, 311 w college. Bd when you get there and I will send you the hotel info"

Charlie: "OK. On way now. Have any sexier pics now?" "Almost there. Are you there are nearby?" "Here"

Agent: "Nearby." "Ur at Albertsons?"

Charlie: "Yea" "yes. Where to"

Agent: "Come to best western on 160" "21382 us 160"

Charlie: "ok" "OK" "OK. Where?"

Agent: "R u here?"

Charlie: "Yes."

Agent: "I'm in the lot and dont see u… Pull in and make a left. I'm standing by my car."

Charlie: "Hi"

Agent: "Hi! That u in van?" "?"

Charlie: "I'm worried to come meet. Why condoms if not needed? Seems like it could be a trap."

Agent: "R u clean? U dont need them if u seem clean."

Charlie: "Maybe being silly." "Am clean."

Agent: "Its not a trap… R u a cop?"

Charlie: "No, just horny but nervous." "We've talked about illegal things, dont want to get out and be in trouble."

Agent: "lol well fuck ur making me nervous… U look like a cop"

Charlie: "Hahaha well if I was I wouldn't be shy about meeting"

Agent: "well hun its cold as fuck out here so lets make a decision soon"

Charlie: "The guy in the car with you too? What do you want me to do?"

Agent: "Here is jus there for my security… Honestly if this isnt for u thats cool but I need to know so I can make some money u kno?"

Charlie: "I wasn't expecting to see somebody else too." "You want to meet out here first??"

Agent: "Yea I understand but he's cool. Just here to make sure u dont rob me."

Charlie: "I understand, worried about my own ass too."

Agent: "Yeah just to make sure u have money and aren't a psycho killer or somethin lol"

Charlie: "When do you want money? Before, after? Never given

money outside and before, before."

Agent: "Before... it is pretty empty over here"

Charlie: "I feel crazy just sitting here." "How do I know they're here?"

Agent: (photo attached)

Charlie: "I'm probably the biggest pita, just havent done this" "I'll come over, but would like to see them before money."

Agent: "I understand sweetie but if u dont want to do this I need to move on to the next date"

Charlie: "You're very patient, I appreciate it" "Can they come to the door or something?"

Agent: "You can see the girls if that would make you feel better. I'd like to meet you first to make sure it cool."

Charlie: "Yes. OK."

The reports went on to say that after this Charlie becomes spooked and leaves. He doesn't message them again, and just drives away. The idea of money first was too far off the normal operating procedure for these exchanges that he left. The police officers pulled him over a block away at a traffic light. The officer called his phone to ensure it was him, and when it rang, they arrested him on the spot. Condoms and enough money for the transaction were in his possession.

Reading this exchange was a hugely pivotal moment for me. It made me physically sick to my stomach. My entire body shaking, sweaty, and my heart racing. This exchange was real to him. He absolutely did intend to go through with sex with an 11 and 14-year-old.

This report also spelled out that this was not a new

experience to him. He knew how far to push the boundaries. He knew the lingo. He knew how things operated normally. He also let in some things that I'm not sure most people who read it would have caught onto.

As much as Charlie kept hidden from me, there were some of his fetishes that I did know about. I knew how arousing he found pregnancy specifically. Early on in our relationship he would often talk about knocking me up, and that would increase his arousal. And then I proceeded to have three children with the man, and he never let it be a secret how sexy he found it. For him, it was not the belly shape or the enlarged breasts, but the mental image of HIS seed being what put me in this state. So when I saw that he was now imagining knocking up these children...well there was no doubt what he was thinking about there.

I really don't know if I would have seen clearly had I been able to read this report before this point or not, but really it didn't matter. I hadn't seen it until now, and once I had, I couldn't unsee it.

Chapter 16

The truth was that up until then I had kept multiple possible outcomes on the table. I had allowed whatever any other expert on this case thought to be a possibility to be a real possibility for the outcome. I even had allowed Charlie's trajectory that we'd figure out how to get back together one day stay open for far too long. I had not yet decided what the ONLY possible outcome was. I had allowed myself to give up that decision and gave all of the power to the systems, the experts, even to Charlie himself, rather than really staying true to everything my intuition had been screaming at me the whole time.

We're told from so young that the experts know better. There's an established hierarchy of parents, teachers, educators, experts—all who know us better than ourselves. Even for punchy kids like I was who did not respect authority like I was told to—some amount of that still sunk in. I got to the point where I was so muddy with possibilities and felt the weight of everyone else's burdens on my shoulders that I couldn't see clearly.

The even harder truth was, I chose to not see clearly. But because it is always a choice on some level, once I recognized it, it was just as easy to open my eyes as it was to shut them in the first place.

Once I was 100% certain of who he was and what had to happen, all of my energy and all of my power were focused in that one direction. Every synchronicity or series of events was dedicated to making that outcome happen. I focused on bringing clarity to the situation so that those that had also seen fog and uncertainty would see with clarity what needed to happen.

I held strong the intention for safety and security for myself and my children. I projected the expectation that the judge would be able to see clearly what was going on here. I just held onto that one and only option to manifest and kept moving forward.

I talked to my lawyers about filing an emergency order called a "Motion to Restrict." The psychic thought that it was important to show the judge how serious I was taking the allegations. There was a possibility it would work, and it would be beneficial to our case if we were in court while parenting time was already restricted.

My lawyers were hesitant. They were really walking the line between being seen as a disgruntled ex-wife and a legitimately concerned mother. They agreed to draft the motion and see what the updated report said. If the recommendation supported it, we would have the ammunition and backup to file it immediately. The way that these motions work is that they are automatically enforced until a hearing is held. I was really hopeful that this would stick.

In the midst of all this preparation, there was another scare. I picked up the boys from Charlie and they had been to the pool for a birthday party with Morgan's children. Now most people wouldn't think much of that, but my first reaction was legitimate concern. I knew that Charlie couldn't have taken them, so I asked who was watching them. I was also immediately worried about Milo not having his floaties at the pool.

When Milo was not even two years old he jumped into the deep end at the pool when my back was turned for an instant. I jumped in after him, only to have him push and fight me to get away. The child truly believed he could breathe underwater. When I took all three boys to the pool, he would walk right into deep water over and over, coughing and spitting up. I could not take my eyes off him for even a second or he'd be under water again. It

was very challenging, especially with two other kids there to watch. So, Milo got floaties. And he was never allowed in water without them.

So when I asked "without your floaties?" with concern it wasn't to try and negate fun he'd had, but real concern. Charlie was angry that I didn't approve of the fun they'd had at the party in some way. I didn't want to fight with him again, so I got the boys in the car and went home.

That night Milo was crying and coughing in his sleep. I went to get him, and he was breathing very fast and labored. I put him in my bed next to me so I could monitor his breathing. I listened to his heart rate and counted his respirations. I searched online for what normal was for an almost five year old and tried to decide whether he was in danger or not.

There is a lot of talk on various mom forums about a phenomenon called secondary drowning. The idea being that if water gets into the lungs and doesn't completely come up, it can cause drowning hours after the incident. I didn't know for sure the validity of the possibility, but seeing labored breathing, fast respirations, and increased heart rate in my child especially after an unknown to me pool visit sent me into a panic. It was one in the morning and I was seriously debating going to the ER.

I texted Charlie, "Did anything happen at the pool today? Did Milo go under the water even for a minute?" I didn't really expect a response—but figured asking might ease my mind.

I watched Milo for another 30 minutes, with no change. No response from Charlie. I'm really not the type of parent to rush to the ER for any reason, but this felt like it warranted medical help.

Eventually at two am I decided it was better to be safe than sorry. Charlie was clearly asleep, and so there wasn't anything to do but wake everyone else up and go. I got the other two boys in the car with their blankets, and

then moved Milo.

We got to the ER and they checked us in right away. They rushed us to a room and started monitoring Milo. The night air seemed to help him some, and he was more awake than he'd been. He was still coughing up a lot of phlegm, but I was grateful that we were getting checked out.

After an hour of monitoring they told us that everything seemed OK, and there was no concern of fluid in his lungs. They recommended steroids for the cough and I agreed. I was so relieved that this was all he needed. I messaged Charlie again letting him know that we had been to the ER, but thankfully everything was OK. I took the boys back home to their beds, relieved.

The next day was Milo's fifth birthday party. I debated canceling it after the visit to the ER. But I was also torn. Punishing him by canceling his party, because I got worried didn't seem fair either. I monitored him that morning and decided that if he wasn't feeling sick or coughing a bunch and had normal respirations, we could keep the party.

I also had Charlie now furious with me that I didn't call him before going to the ER. Except I did message him, and he was clearly asleep. I spoke to the evaluator about why I took him in and explained Milo's history at the pool. It didn't take her long to recognize again what this was. Anything I did was wrong in Charlie's eyes, including being concerned enough to take three kids to the ER in the middle of the night because one of them was having serious trouble breathing.

We got her report back and this time the evaluation was even more extensive. There wasn't the same history of the relationship, as that was all contained in the first report, but there was another 52 pages of evidence with detailed accounts of every fight Charlie and I had had over the last three months. And even better, there was a

new diagnosis for him—Passive Aggressive Personality Disorder. *Well, it wasn't that fitting. Because fuck, wasn't he ever?*

The evaluator had also interviewed the Durango police officer and received his version of events as well as the case file itself. The officer had no doubt about Charlie's original intentions, and had no doubt that I was absolutely a legitimately concerned mother.

She interviewed probation about the polygraph that they had done to supposedly clear him of the finger sucking incident. She had access to the records that I didn't. The polygraph only questioned him on whether or not he touched or was aroused by Alex's privates. There were zero questions regarding anything about finger sucking or even whether finger sucking was arousing to him. Even she was shocked at their incompetence and follow through.

I had started seeing a different therapist at the recommendation of my lawyer due to all the escalation happening, this time choosing someone who was specifically versed in trauma. She was also quoted in the report officially diagnosing me with PTSD due to how long the symptoms had been persisting. Finally seeing the truth of what happened and navigating multiple traumatic events was keeping my nervous system into overdrive. I was living in a constant state of fight or flight.

I immensely appreciated the report. It included everything and more of what had been going on with my children.

At the same time, the recommendation was still to give Charlie some parenting time.

This time it was recommended that I have sole decision-making; all decisions would be made solely by me. She felt I did not need to have to navigate the intense personality disorders anymore regarding major decisions. The conflict between us had gone from mild to

what was now considered moderate to severe, and all decisions about the children were being used as ammunition.

She did now recommend he have less parenting time, down to only every other weekend plus one day. What was particularly interesting about this was that her reasoning was actually protective of me. She felt if he only had supervised time that he would use that one-to-two hour window to further alienate the children from me, leaving me the bad guy for taking away their father.

Her goal in giving him some time was to try and mitigate that possibility and still keep my relationship with the children as strong as possible.

There was another large list of recommendations for family counseling, individual counseling, and a parenting time coordinator that were also listed.

My attorneys felt the content in the report was enough. They knew that getting a recommendation for only supervised time was nearly impossible, but the background data in this one was much stronger than the first. Even more importantly, the report showed that his mental health was deteriorating not improving. Additionally, we had evidence now that he either was not capable or not willing to follow any of the court recommendations. The distinction was irrelevant. The point was that he didn't, despite what it meant for his parenting time.

We filed the motion to restrict within an hour of the report coming out. It was normally a Charlie pickup day, so I left work early to intercept and get them from school before they would normally walk the two blocks off campus to meet him. To say I was not scared to run into him would be a lie. I stayed calm, and I had a plan. I took the boys to a grocery store outside of city limits and bought them a special treat. We were going to make an

adventure out of the change in routine. I was sensitive to the confusion that they would feel. Axel and Ethan especially really struggled if they didn't know their plan ahead of time. I also didn't want to give them details about what was going on, because truthfully, I didn't know 100% that the motion would stick.

By dinner time it looked like the judge had accepted it. She confirmed that we'd discuss this and the final orders in court on the same day. There was no other court date filed. *Holy fuck it worked.* I was in near disbelief and extremely grateful at the same time.

I told the kids that they would be staying with just me for a bit. Axel was worried about his soccer practice. His stuff was at Charlie's. I told him we'd get new things and that either I could take him, or he could take the school bus if he wanted. He liked that idea a lot; he had friends that rode the school bus and it sounded exciting. I told him I'd see if I could work out those details tomorrow, but we'd figure it out.

The next morning, Charlie's lawyer filed another motion. This time he was trying to dismantle the automatic restriction of my motion. He wanted to know whether that was intentional on the judge's part or not. My lawyer didn't feel that was going to make much of a difference, but I was nervous. Something wasn't right here, but we couldn't exactly refuse them that clarification.

Two hours later the judge stated that there would be no change to parenting time. She was going to hear both sides in court. *Fuck. Here we go again.* This was a moment for me that I began to question myself. *Was I doing the right thing here? Why was this so hard? What was I missing? Was it just too late? No, no I couldn't accept that. I had to stay strong. I had to hold true to MY truth.*

Sometimes, when we're working towards a goal we run into roadblocks. Truthfully, it's more than

sometimes, it's every time. There is always something that happens that we didn't expect. Something that we didn't account for, or something that gets in the way of what we're trying to accomplish. And our very human reaction is to give up. Throw our hands in the air and proclaim, "It wasn't meant to be." I mean come on—if it was just that easy wouldn't everyone have everything they wanted?

It's not easy, and it's never predictable. What I have come to understand is that it's not even a test really that the universe is throwing us, it's more about the fact that changing directions so drastically isn't instantaneous. Manifesting what we want when it impacts others takes a lot of movement. It takes mass amounts of inspiration and guidance and FOLLOWING THROUGH.

So, if I had given up and stopped pushing, would I be where I am today? Maybe, but I doubt it. Instead, I had a good cry, and came to the conclusion that there was another reason it wasn't time to restrict yet. I had to trust myself and my ability to stay true to what I was creating for myself. I had to trust that this was happening FOR ME, not to me. More data was required. Something else still needed to happen. *I just had to keep my eyes open to pick it up and trust that it was all going exactly as it needed to.*

The other big change that this brought about was that I began to see my children with more clarity too. Rather than being frustrated with their behavior I saw all the ways that they were just as confused as I had been. They too had so many feelings and ideas about what they wanted to happen, and as kids they really needed stability and comfort from their parental figures. They didn't understand the emotions they were picking up around them. They hated that grownups continued to keep secrets from them, but most of all they just wanted to feel safe.

So, I began to become really focused on safety with

the boys. I sat and read with them every night I could. I spent longer amounts of time with each of them individually tucking them in, checking in with their day. I really tried to listen for what they needed and read in between the lines of what they were saying Daddy said or what happened at Daddy's house. Every time it came up, I recorded the conversation. This was not something that was their fault. Blame needed to be placed where it was due and nowhere else.

It was now about two weeks before court. I sat down with them to read a book about body safety. It was a book about red flags and keeping bodies safe. This was a protective measure that I wanted to make sure they understood to keep asking for help if the first grownup wasn't listening. The book is *A Child to Child's Guide to Keeping Private Parts Private*. It tells a story where a boy is at a sleepover and he isn't comfortable with what he is being asked to do by some other kids, and so he hides in the bathroom until everyone falls asleep and then calls his mom to come get him.

But the book also went through and talked about other red flags—other reasons that kids would need to ask for help. If anyone asked to see their privates, if anyone touched their privates. Then the book goes on to say that if someone shows you pictures or videos where there are naked people, that's also a red flag.

Axel stopped me here, "Well, but it's OK if it's animated, right?

Fuck. I breathed and tried to stay calm.

"Why do you ask, buddy? Has someone shown you anything like this before?"

Silence...He shut down. I dropped it. Another thing to bring up with my attorney and the evaluator. It was bedtime anyway. I tucked Milo in first.

Axel was second. He was still thinking about the book we had read. He said the little boy was smart to hide in

the bathroom. I agreed. He was thinking about where his friends lived, in relation to our houses. He wanted to make sure he had his own escape plan ready just in case. I told him no matter what time it was, if he called me, I would come get him, even if it was two am. That made him feel better too.

I then had the idea to ask him what the sleeping arrangements were like at Daddy's house. I set my phone on his nightstand and hit record. I knew he had recently been moved into his own room downstairs, away from his brothers. He confirmed that, but he also said he usually slept with Daddy on the couch or in Daddy's bed.

"Oh, well why is that?"

"That's where Daddy sleeps."

"Does Daddy ever sleep in your bed with you?"

"Yes, sometimes."

"Does he do that with your brothers too?"

"No, just me."

I tucked him into bed and kissed him goodnight.

That motherfucker. I was angry, terrified really, but stayed calm. In my house Axel, who was now seven, had been sleeping in his own bed just fine. Milo would often sneak into my bed at some point in the night, but he was four, and he still always started the night in his room. This was the other piece of evidence I clearly needed. I hated that it had come to this, but here we were.

With now less than two weeks till court, there was no filing any more motions—the only thing I had to do was be patient. I was meeting with my attorney next week to go over court preparation. My mom was also flying in to come to support me for court. She would be here in less than a week.

My mom arrived on a Friday night—a week before our court date. I was grateful to have her support here, knowing this was going to be intense for everyone.

The next morning, I woke up to my work email on

my phone not being available. I also couldn't log into anything remotely which was really odd so I went into work to check on everything, leaving my mom sleeping in my guest room. I figured it was something easy and I would be home fast and spend the day with my mom before picking up the boys that evening.

Well, time for another curveball. My office had just been the target of a ransomware encryption attack. I could not connect or log into anything, even at the office. We had been infiltrated and literally every machine that was turned on was now encrypted. All authentication servers, application servers, everything. Even our cloud platforms were encrypted. Remember here, I was the IT Manager, so this was strictly my domain and entirely my problem. I called Marcus to come in and help me evaluate the damage. *Holy mother of fuck.*

I spent the entire day at work with Marcus, my boss, and the CEO. This was massive. We were going to have to rebuild every single computer. We were quickly checking and verifying offline backups to verify whether we needed to pay the ransom or not. We were hopeful but had to be 100% certain before the clock on the ransom ran out. The plan was that everyone had to come back in on Sunday, and they were going to figure out a manual operations process to get us through until we were back up. Buckle up, it was about to be a busy couple of weeks. And I still had court to prepare for. Talk about a big ass test of willpower.

My mom helped me with the boys a ton that week. I had to be at work as much as I possibly could to get things back up and running. We had hired outside support to get us up as efficiently as we could, but we were essentially shoving over a year of rebuilding 300+ computers into just a week. Every single desktop, laptop, server, or device on the network had to be wiped and rebuilt. As a global company with six locations, four in

the US, and two in Europe—that was a lot.

I have to say while this might have broken some people, for me it was such a welcome distraction from what would have been an impossible week to get through. I was in a weird sort of way grateful for the timing. I was already enough of a stress case every time the boys left to go to Charlie's—leading up to court wasn't going to be any easier—the pressure was just intensifying. But now, I had more than enough on my plate to keep me solely focused elsewhere.

I don't know that everyone would have reacted that way to MORE stress on their plate, but for me that is true. We have to look for the blessings where we can find them and take a step back to see the bigger picture when things come our way that we didn't expect. So, I pushed forward. I worked a 60+ hour week, and took off just to meet my lawyer for court preparations.

My lawyers put me on the stand in their office to practice what opposing counsel might throw at me. They picked apart my story and my point of view. I was firm, I was strong. Charlie had also found out that I had listed him as "Pedo" in my phone, which my lawyers thought was maybe the only thing valid they had to throw at me. We talked about the mental health difficulties I was going through, and that my children didn't have any access to my phone, and if they did in the future, I had learned my lesson and removed it. We practiced until they felt that I was not going to be thrown by anything said from the other side.

We also went extensively over what the plan was in court. As the respondent I went second. The Evaluator was going to be a major part of our case. She was key as she was able to be certified as an expert witness. Her opinion held a ton of weight and we already knew how she felt as it was in the report.

We had a couple of additional witnesses, including

the police officer that I had been working with, and that had been Charlie's arresting officer. He was going to certify the accuracy of the police report I had received. Another witness was the old supervisor that used to try and facilitate a parenting agreement between Charlie and I and witnessed him verbally attacking me.

The other goal was to invalidate Charlie's support team. We knew his therapist and probation officer would be called—and we also knew that they were not experts and did not even follow their own protocol with him. They openly did not enforce many of his probation terms and conditions. Because he paid the probation bill, they did not require him to be employed, despite what the terms of probation outlined. He claimed he was a stay-at-home parent when the children were all in school. They did not once check his devices for pornography. In fact, after he moved, it took them over six months to visit his new place. It was pure incompetence, and we were going to let them dig their own grave with that.

I shared what had happened with Axel the week prior, and we added to the list of things that they were going to bring through my testimony. It was hearsay certainly, but my lawyer was ready for that. It showed my state of mind and explained my actions. Not claimed as truth, but as MY truth was enough. We were almost certain the judge would want to hear it and let it through.

We were ready, as ready as we could be. I wasn't going to work at all that day. It was just about focusing on manifesting everything I needed to happen. Believing that the judge would see the situation clearly. That my children would be seen as in danger of the situation getting much much worse. That I would be seen as a protective parent, not an alienating one. That finally protection would be put in place so that I could breathe easily again and start to move on with my life.

It was time.

Chapter 17

The day had come. It had all been leading up to this. I woke up and ran on my treadmill, and did my best to clear my head. I ate a light breakfast, and got dressed. I was ready.

I was supposed to meet my lawyer at his office that morning, so my mom was driving separately. It seemed that the entire legal office had been preparing for today. Most of them were getting prepped to come to the courthouse with us.

My lawyer and I walked into the courtroom and my mom and my support friend/coworker, Kate, were already there. They looked up and smiled at me. I knew that I had so much support here both physically and energetically. I knew my angels and newfound spirit friends were by my side. This was a big day for everyone. We took our seats in the front.

My lawyer took out the evidence binders. My stack was a fully packed three-inch binder. Charlie's was a small stack of stapled papers. The evaluator's reports filled another one-inch binder. The difference between them all was striking. No stone was left unturned; I made certain of that.

Charlie's mom and friend were the only ones on the other side of the courtroom. They were quiet and didn't even look up at me.

My lawyer repeated again what the plan was. We had to time both sides, as the judge would keep us on track that way. Each side had three-and-a-half hours to make their case. My lawyer expected most of it to be taken up by the evaluator, but they also had to cross Charlie and his witnesses and save enough time for me. Other than the evaluator, my testimony was the most important.

The door opened behind me and I didn't even look back. I knew it was him. I could feel the energy in the room shift, but there was no way I was going to let him affect me in any way today. I focused on setting my intentions that anything he projected onto me would just reflect back on him like he had big giant mirrors all around him. I felt into the presence of everyone who'd supported me this far. Deep breath. I had this.

Charlie and his lawyer took their seats, and the judge walked in. It was time to begin.

Opening statements were repeated versions of what we'd talked about in the motions. We believed the children were in danger now, today. We believed that Charlie's mental health was only deteriorating and that he was either incapable, or unwilling to comply with what was required to ensure that the children were safe and cared for. His side believed I was overreacting. I was angry that he filed for divorce. That I was only trying to punish Charlie for what happened. They claimed what I had done wrong was just as bad.

The evaluator was called to the stand first. First the evaluator was certified as an expert witness. It was fairly standard since her role was appointed by the court, but it was an important formality. Her testimony needed to carry more weight than the others. Charlie's lawyer was going to have a particularly hard time here since there was SO much evidence directly from her against him. They tried to pull apart the times that she sided with me. They felt that it was a double standard and that I did things that weren't in the children's best interest also. We were equal. This had been his defense all along. False equivalence. No one is perfect, so if you shine a light on someone's insecurities and they back down, you win.

It didn't work—the evaluator saw right through it. She clearly stated that I acted appropriately given what had been going on. My actions were entirely expected

behaviors from someone who had experienced the type of trauma that I did. I was in therapy and was working on what I needed to do. I also did everything asked of me by the evaluator while working full-time and raising three boys. Charlie on the other hand did absolutely zero of the requested actions.

My lawyer stepped up. He crafted his questions carefully. Could a person with addictive tendencies be grooming? Could dependent personality disorder look like grooming? Could a person with these disorders not even know what they were doing? Could a person with these mental health issues have trouble with boundaries? Could they have trouble knowing what inappropriate even looked like? Did someone with this history and these traits be a danger to their children? It went on and on and on and every question set up more of the conclusion we needed from her. There needed to be no question from the judge that the most qualified person in the room agreed that my children were in danger TODAY. With Charlie's history and his actions, was he a potential danger? Was he potentially grooming his children? The answer was always yes.

My lawyer sat back down. His boss, and named partner at the firm looks at me and says, "That was the best damn cross I've seen of a PRE[3] in 40 years." It truly was a spectacular performance.

Next, they quickly called the supervisor who witnessed our attempt at mediating parenting time. Charlie's side didn't do more than confirm she had given great reports about Charlie with the children while he was out on bond. Our goal was different. We brought up the parenting time mediation attempt and his hyper fixation on me that she witnessed. She validated our concerns. The case was definitely building.

---

[3] Parental rights evaluator.

Everyone else was going to have to be after lunch. I walked to lunch with my mom and Kate. We were feeling positive. Not overconfident but positive. This was a really good start.

After lunch was Charlie's sex offender treatment therapist. My mom, who is a very well-educated mental health professional, was SHOCKED when his therapist walked to the stand. She told me later she was SHOCKED that he was in charge of sex offenders. "That's the guy?" She was appalled and flabbergasted.

For a mental health professional, he was completely unsure with his words, and he did not hold Charlie accountable as he cited the program as the excuse. He believed Charlie was low risk and in full compliance. My lawyers successfully crossed, and he did not certify as an expert witness. Anything he was saying was merely his opinion in the eyes of the court. This was good. They pointed out all the holes in the program. They pointed out the holes in the questions asked by the polygraphs. It was really quite sad if it wasn't so infuriating that this man was in charge of all sex offenders in our small county.

Next was his parole officer. She had a similar aura around her. She was cocky and full of ego. Again, it was the policy of her department not to enforce employment if the bills were paid. He didn't break any outward rules, so they didn't feel it necessary to check on him further. All the excuses in the world, and yet he was still considered exceptionally compliant. She too did not certify as an expert witness in the case. Our point was made.

Next was Charlie's turn. He was the last witness for his side. He rambled on and on about how hard it has been. About how much he's tried to work with me. About how I wouldn't negotiate with him because court was coming. He took up their entire time saying basically

nothing. He looked miserable, greasy, and very much like a predator. Everything he said was just reaffirming our case. He could not have made it any easier for us. He rambled on so much he left his lawyer with only five minutes left to cross me.

We on the other hand had about 30 minutes left. Cross of Charlie's witnesses took longer than we hoped, but we were determined to fit in an hour of testimony in 30 minutes. I could be fast, we had practiced. Short concise answers unless he asked for more clarification. Perfect.

I got on the stand. My heart was racing—this was going to have to be good. I was the key to bringing forward everything that had not been in the evaluator's report. I was going to have to bring forth the finger sucking event, the Axel behavior, the sleeping arrangements, everything.

I stayed calm, I kept my attention on the judge and not the audience. I wanted her to see exactly what Axel showed me. I wanted her to hear my fear and my determination to protect my children. I wanted there to be no question in her mind what needed to happen.

My lawyer asked multiple times for me to show the judge exactly how Axel moved his fingers in his mouth for the judge. She watched me every time. We brought forward the case file that had just been unsealed. I had only just received the truth of what happened in 2016. I didn't have the information when I had supported him after the arrest. I believed the story he told me. But seeing it now, the conversation with the undercover agent was undeniable. He not only asked for both the 11 and 14-year-olds, but he wanted it to be recorded, and he even fantasized about impregnating them. I had three kids with the man, I knew all about his pregnancy fetish.

I knew what I was doing was going to shock the judge. That was my intent. Be clear, respectful, honest, and

make there be not a shadow of doubt about what had been transpiring. My lawyer played both recordings from Axel. Both were admitted into evidence as explanations of my behavior. The judge was eager to hear what had been going on.

We addressed every concern from the other side. I admitted to any behavior they questioned. I also showed where I recognized my actions and corrected them. I took accountability where it was due.

We had quick short questions, and answers. We successfully got everything we needed across in record time. The performance was again phenomenal. No one in that courtroom could question why I was doing what I did. No one could possibly question my motives. This was only about my children and keeping them safe.

Closing arguments were made. Neither side had any time, but we didn't care. We said all of what we needed to and kept it short. Ethan was in danger NOW, Axel was in danger NOW, Milo was in danger NOW—and unless this court did something to stop it, things were only going to get worse.

Now it was the judge's turn. We knew it was very unlikely that she would make a ruling today, that almost never happened. She has to go over an entire day of testimony and all of our documents in order to do that, but what we didn't expect was for her to show her hand either.

She very clearly ordered Charlie NOT to sleep with any of the children at all. That was way over the line from her viewpoint. He was to not discuss the case with them at all either. They shouldn't even know that their parents were in court. I could tell she wanted to say more but held it back. She had to release us and go through it all to make her determination.

We left the courtroom on a high. We didn't know anything for sure yet, but we definitely rocked that trial

to the best of our combined abilities. I was so grateful for everyone's support. They reminded me again that all the evidence wasn't stuff they tracked down—it was all me. I did it. I created this opening and this possibility for my children to have some security. They were right.

We went out to dinner to celebrate. I invited Marcus and Greg and my mom. It was good to get out and breathe and know that no matter what happened I had been thorough.

Tuesday night (only four days after court) my lawyer called me at 6:30 pm. The order had just come in. He was sending it over to me and wanted me to read it over first and then he would call me back.

I had just gotten home from work. I sat down and opened my email. The order was 18 pages long. It described everything that had happened in court. It pointed out every place that Charlie had not complied. The judge had made a plan.

She ordered that immediately his time be reduced to only two afternoons a week, Monday and Friday 3-7pm. He would have six weeks to comply with ALL of her requirements and if he did so, he would receive the evaluators recommended every other weekend and a day. If he did not comply with the recommendations, he would only be allowed supervised parenting time. If 120 days passed and he still had not complied, then supervised parenting time would be the permanent parenting plan. I had 100% decision-making either way.

My reaction was primarily relief. It was not exactly what we asked for, but it was WAY better than where we were currently at. And at least in the short term, no more overnights meant there was a huge amount of safety being put in place. Part of me truly suspected that Charlie was not unwilling, but incapable of compliance, and it was only a matter of time before the supervised time was enacted.

The following day was not only my day to pick up the kids, but was my 33rd birthday. My finalized divorce with new protections in place for my children was the best birthday present I could have ever asked for.

We had an appointment already scheduled with their therapist; it was perfect timing. We had discussed telling them all together with her present so that there was support for everyone. I knew that they were going to have questions.

The change in behavior in my children was almost immediate. Even my mom noticed a shift the last couple of days she was there. The intensity died down. They still were quite obstinate and combative, but the chaos started to subside.

We were going to be OK.

Chapter 18

I had not had the boys home with me longer than a couple of days in over a year, and really wanted to take them to do something fun over spring break. It was assigned as my year and that meant they would be with me for nine whole days! After Morgan befriended Charlie, I had reconnected with my old friend Greg, her now ex-husband, and I decided to take the boys to go up to Denver with him and his two children. We had both been through a lot over the last couple of years. It was going to be a great change of pace.

What I didn't expect was for a global pandemic to shut the country down that week. March of 2020 turned out to be the beginning of a very different world. When we got back from Denver, all the schools were shutting down, and my job immediately went remote.

I could not believe the timing of it all. If we hadn't succeeded when we did, there was a high chance of the boys being in quarantine with Charlie, not to mention the continued fighting over every little thing. The pandemic brought custody battles to a whole new level for so many families.

The six weeks from our court date went by quickly. I was enjoying spending more time with the boys even with the chaos of remote school and work. We began reconnecting differently. We had breakfast and lunch together every day. We figured out a sort of semblance of a schedule for schooling and it mostly was working.

With school now remote, I dropped off the boys at Charlie's house at three pm and picked them up at the grocery store near my home at seven pm. Some of their favorite nighttime items moved back over to my house so they could feel secure in the bedrooms again. They did

not question me on why they couldn't spend the night with Dad anymore. I believe on some level they were relieved to feel settled.

Everyone's behavior shifted. I noticed how much more calm the household was. Ethan, the biggest introvert, was thriving in this new setting. He was still getting work done, but able to also focus on things he enjoyed like learning to code and other educational games.

Axel missed his friends, but also was enjoying the new neighborhood. We had a small pond and trails a short distance from the house. We went on outdoor adventures just the four of us as much as we could.

Milo was happy to do whatever his brothers were doing. They would play LEGO® together, build forts, and play out in the yard.

A couple of hours before the scheduled afternoon switch off, on the Friday afternoon before the Order of Compliance to the court was due, Charlie sent me a message saying he had a runny nose. He wanted to take all precautions and asked if I wanted to keep the boys with me instead. I happily agreed.

That list of things that he was supposed to do to comply with the court? Not a single one had been accomplished. No letter of compliance was filed with the court. That evening I removed all future scheduled times from the shared parenting calendar. Parenting time would have to be scheduled and supervised from here on out.

One of the requirements that he didn't comply with from the very beginning was disclosure about his felony offense to the boys. It actually was the original reason we sought out therapy for them, as they would often ask questions and we wanted to be careful with how we gave answers. Their therapist always said that ideally the disclosure comes from Dad directly, but the only script

he ever provided she felt was inappropriately detailed for their ages. I had been waiting for Charlie to tell them more, because I agreed the specifics would be best coming from him, as I also knew they would have so many questions for him afterwards.

It had been something I had been trying to get him to do for over a year. They knew that Daddy was in trouble, but they didn't know why. They knew he couldn't be around other kids, but again they didn't know why. I knew that as they got older it would be increasingly important. I did not want their first disclosure to be a kid in middle school who googled Ethan's parents. This was the age of the internet, and not telling them when there were news articles out there was completely irresponsible.

Because so much time had passed with this particular avoidance, I had been working with my therapist on my own version of a script for them. I knew that at some point it was actually going to be up to me to tell them the truth and I wanted to be ready.

My script was very simple:

"You guys have had a lot of questions over the last couple of years about why Daddy is in trouble and what happened. I want to give you guys the best answers I can and please ask questions if you don't understand what I'm saying.

You guys know a lot about rules, and rules at home and at school and rules in the community that are called laws. There are lots of different kinds of laws, but the ones I want to talk about are laws about keeping kids safe. Remember the red flag book I was reading you guys? Those red flags are all things that are against the law.

Daddy is in trouble because Daddy was trying to do things with children that would hurt them. He wanted to touch them in a way that grown-ups are not allowed to touch kids. He wanted to touch their private parts and do

things that only grown-ups are allowed to do with other grown-ups. This is why he cannot be around other children right now.

What Daddy did was against the law and he was caught by the police. He's on a grown up timeout that is called probation through the court system and their job is to check on him to make sure he follows all of his rules. It's very important for Daddy to keep following all of his rules.

You guys need to know that if Daddy ever tried to touch you in a way that made you feel weird at all, that you would need to tell Tara[4] or your school counselor, and Mommy so that we can make sure to help you and also get Daddy the help he needs too. Daddy has a sickness that some grownups have; and he sometimes doesn't know what is right or wrong.

Daddy loves you all very much, and wants you guys to know that he is working on getting better."

I ended up having to have separate conversations with each one of them. They all needed a different level of processing to what I was saying.

As soon as I started, Ethan ran away and didn't want to hear the message. Axel cried and said that didn't seem like Daddy. I held him and told him I was just as surprised when I learned the truth. Milo latched onto the idea that he has a sickness and so that explained it to him well enough. They all processed it very differently. I knew that as time went on, they'd have more questions and I'd do everything I could to be as age sensitive, but truthful as I could be.

Charlie sent a message the following Monday asking to talk to the boys. I had told them he wasn't feeling great and so they were skipping their regular Friday afternoon with him. They talked for a bit about their day. Axel and Ethan's birthdays were coming up, but with COVID no

---

[4] Their therapist.

one was having a party. There was sadness in Charlie's eyes, but I also sensed some amount of relief.

He asked to call again on Axel's birthday and then again on Ethan's. They were both occupied with their new gifts and showing them off. The conversation was simple and neither of them asked when they'd see him again. They didn't bring up the disclosure I had made to them either. After 30 minutes or so they hung up.

The boys and I didn't hear anything from Charlie after that. No contact whatsoever since those calls in April of 2020. No request for visitation, no child support payments, no phone calls, or emails. He hasn't sent one single message. At first, I was terrified that more was coming. But then that July deadline also came and went—the 120-day mark now passed with still nothing. That was it. To regain any form of custody would be immensely more difficult for him now. The fight was over. The kids were with me 100% and we were all finally truly safe.

Taking a deep breath felt different from this place. The safety and security I had held intentions for so strongly manifested in a way I truly did not expect. After all that fighting, it just stopped.

My nervous system took some time to regulate. I had been living in fight or flight for years and years. I didn't even know what being not stressed looked or felt like.

I found myself still terrified of the little things. Driving around town, I would watch every vehicle so closely just in case it might be his. Since we were also smack in the middle of the pandemic I was grocery shopping online and utilizing delivery or pick-up, but another part of me was terrified that we might even run into him at the store. I had no clue how I might respond to him or the children if that were to happen and I really did not want to find out.

I was constantly looking over my shoulder for the next shoe to drop, even though there were no more shoes.

For a short while I let myself believe that it was my angel guides that saved me. That they facilitated these series of events so that I would finally be safe.

Now whether you believe in angels or spirits or not, it really doesn't matter, as the truth was that ***everything shifted for me once I let go of the indecision and truly made a choice.*** That's what that session did for me, it showed me how important it was for me to finally choose for me.

And so now that all of it was over I began searching for more connection, more answers, and more understanding. I didn't want to live in fear of something else happening down the road. I wanted to learn how to get answers for myself. To trust myself more completely.

I had experienced the power of standing in my truth, but now that we were safe—what would we do next?

Chapter 19

The pandemic continued to shift my life in ways I didn't expect. When my office went remote, it meant that my job eventually became more challenging to do with three kids homeschooling. While they did have some schoolwork, they needed support and supervision. As time passed the excitement of school from home wore off, and they were much less enthused by the assignments. Summer was here and so we decided to focus on play.

My job offered me paid leave through the updated FMLA act, and I took it. I had been struggling with my manager who expected me to begin to micromanage my now remote team, and my personality and beliefs no longer melded well with the role I was being asked to fulfill. I could write a whole other book about what transpired leading up to and after the encryption attack, but the relevant part for this story is that after the three months were up, I didn't go back.

So there I was all of a sudden completely untethered. No job, no ex-husband, and in a pandemic with not much social interaction either. It was a version of freedom I had never experienced before. Just me and my boys navigating our new life together.

I continued searching. I began learning more of who I actually am and why this experience happened to me. I explored spirituality with an openness that I had not done before.

I realized if other people have this connection to more out there, why couldn't I? Big existential questions ran through me as I tried to make sense of what had happened.

Massive traumatic events are often the catalyst to spiritual awakenings, and mine was absolutely that. The truth of the universe was bigger than I had previously allowed myself to explore and now I wanted to find out more.

I jumped into learning everything that interested me. Quantum energy healing was one of them, and through classes I found myself making new connections with people all over the world.

I also knew I would eventually need to leave Durango. I had spent 15 years there, and now there wasn't anything left for me. I had friends, sure, and Marcus was still sometimes around, but I could feel the town constricting my movement and expansion. The possibility of ever running into Charlie was quite probable as the town was small with only 20,000 people inside city limits. Even after the panic subsided, that thought was unacceptable to me—we would have to leave.

There was no rush as the pandemic offered a layer of protection. Everyone was home now, everyone stayed isolated. I had time to sort through it all and start to make some decisions.

I focused everything I did on my healing and the boy's healing. I wanted to understand more about how energy worked in our bodies and our minds. I wanted to ensure that the ancestral patterns that were passed down to me, didn't pass further onto them. I knew that the more work I did on myself, the more opportunity they would have to thrive.

My spiritual growth accelerated very, very quickly. I loved the new understanding I was getting, and I loved learning new ways to help support people who had been through big traumas like I had.

It shocked me to learn how many women end up sharing custody with their abusers or their children's

abusers. There is very little support for women in those situations. Money is a huge determinant in many cases of who wins and who loses. My own divorce, with all the difficulty, cost me over $75,000. Those without financial resources have an even bigger battle ahead of them.

Knowing that I won my case, even just in part, because I had access to those resources set off a fire in me to do something more about it. The first step being writing out this story you're reading now.

I really started to see that what I did that day in the office with the psychic was such a shift in energy that I essentially leaped into a completely new reality for myself. *I had collapsed a huge pattern by standing up to Charlie. And by doing that, it was actually me who created the outcome I needed for myself and my children.*

All the pieces started clicking together for me. I was learning how to be empowered to get answers from within myself, because truly that's where all the answers were in the first place. I just didn't know how to listen.

The most important thing that I did during that entire ordeal was that I stopped giving away my power and my energy to the systems and specialists, and I started to instead use it to create my reality for myself. Once I did that, all I had to do was follow through on every synchronicity or nudge that came to me. By trusting myself so completely to create that experience, I all but guaranteed that the outcome would be in my favor.

That fall, Milo, who was now five, stormed into my room one morning demanding to know why he couldn't talk to Daddy. Why wouldn't I let him call? I explained that Daddy made his own choices, and that Daddy knew what he was supposed to do in order to get to spend time with him. Daddy also knew what the consequences were if he didn't, and still he made that choice.

I will never forget the immediate look of understanding and betrayal on my five-year old's face

when he finally got that. It was truly heartbreaking. "I hate Daddy!" He cried in my lap. I have repeated time and time again that Daddy made his own choices and that it has never been something that I did, or they did. Daddy has a sickness, and it has only ever been his choice for how he chooses to get help with it or not.

That is true for all of us. We all have choices every day. Recognizing that in every moment, there is in fact a choice, is a very powerful realization.

I had the choice to stay in the marriage, to support my husband through his offense, despite all the evidence suggesting it was not a safe idea. I had the choice to support him so much I brought him back home and into our lives. I had the choice to go back to work, and to begin dating. I had the choice every time to not see what was right in front of me.

And I also had the choice to stop doing all of that and finally see clearly what had been in front of me the entire time. Once I did, it was only a decision from me that was going to change what was beginning to transpire.

The most shocking thing to most people when they hear parts of my story is just how difficult this was. He is a felon who tried to have sex with an 11 and 14-year-old, and yet you still had to go through all that?

Unfortunately, the answer is yes.

I had no idea when it all began just how difficult supporting him would be to undo. I was so wrapped up in "fixing" the family for everyone else I didn't stop to consider what was actually in everyone's best interest. I could not see any other possibility other than supporting him and putting whatever semblance of a family back together. That was my entire world and I refused to allow it to completely crumble.

My husband was finally paying attention to me in a way I had always wanted. I wanted nothing more than to keep my family together. I chose to trust his side of the

story, and believe that he was a safe man. All of that made it very difficult for me to see what was going on under the surface.

There is an assumption in the criminal and family court system that victims all know when they are being abused or lied to. There was an assumption that I would have left and not supported him if there was any danger to my children. There was and still is zero recognition of what trauma situations look like and when trauma bonding actually happens.

I had developed a unique bond with Charlie going through this ordeal completely isolated from the outside world.

One of the most difficult parts of this whole story for people to understand is what our relationship looked like while he was on bond. I had completely isolated myself from everyone around me. The only person who understood what I was going through was Charlie himself. There was no one else to talk to—no one else who could possibly understand. My family tried to reach out but all I felt from them was judgment. How could they not understand that I HAD to support my husband? My mom even suggested that I move to Oregon even temporarily to be closer to my sister. *How dare she!? She took MY dad away; I was not doing that to my kids.*

Charlie and I went through a second honeymoon of sorts. We saw each other as much as we could, given all the restrictions. We both felt safe inside the bubble of just us. No one else could possibly understand—I don't think we even understood. Because it was so hard to spend time together, that's all we wanted to do.

We were literally talking on the phone almost 24/7. He was in my ear and in my head at all times.

He became a part of every single conversation I had with myself. I had no idea the psychological effect that was having on me. I had no sense of sovereignty over self.

It was only we and us, never I.

I told myself that I was helping him stay connected to the boys. We were keeping the family together since we couldn't be together. I was also so scared to actually FEEL what had happened. If the feeling creeped up, I stuffed them back down so fast—*no we were not dealing with that now*. And Charlie was absolutely terrified to allow me to be on my own for even a minute. If I had a moment to myself with my own thoughts, it was likely I'd come to my senses and so he did everything possible to make sure I didn't.

This type of dynamic is eerily similar to what kidnappers do to their victims. They isolate them—they only allow them contact with one person. Only one person understands them. Only one person gets it. Everything wrong in their life—only one person—the one who caused the pain—is the one they can turn to.

It's a form of trauma bonding and that's exactly what was going on between Charlie and I. Keeping that bubble —the one with me and him against the world—became my only focus as much as it was his. He was terrified I'd wake up one day and see the truth and change my mind and so his entire purpose became focused on keeping me away from everyone else around me. And I was terrified that my children were going to grow up without a father, just as I had.

All my early support and the fact that the family court system in Colorado rarely makes an exception to awarding 50/50 shared custody made the legal battle what it was. Even in cases like mine, where there is a proven history, I had to ultimately prove that grooming and alienating behavior was not only taking place with my own children, but that it was heading down a further dangerous path, for my concerns to be taken seriously.

Both the criminal and family court systems are not protective in any way. They only serve as punitive for the

actions that have already taken place. The actions have to be bad enough. The truth is any protection for our children must come from the parents. It is our role to stand up and speak for our children who don't have the voices to do so.

I believed that my husband was a safe person. That there was a misunderstanding. Everything I had done up until that point had been about keeping my family safe and well cared for. I was living in a space where there wasn't a choice to do anything differently. It did not occur to me even once to leave. It did not occur to me to do anything but support him through it.

I believed that the only way my children would be OK was if I kept the family together. I had built up in my mind that it was my responsibility to do that and that meant staying and supporting their father through anything that was thrown at me.

I believed that if they had their father in their lives, they would be OK, and if they were OK, nothing else mattered, and I would be OK too. It was convoluted, and yet I think that there are a whole lot of women out there who think the same thing I did.

I believed that Charlie's best options for healing and rehabilitation were if I stayed with him. The support I gave him meant he wasn't going through his demons alone. He would want to dissect what happened, his thought processes, and the dangerous thought patterns that led him to visiting prostitutes. He would talk to me like I was his therapist, when in actuality I was his wife, and his biggest victim.

I built up this idea that I could in fact help him heal. I could help him get through the self-loathing, and help him begin to take accountability for his actions. I took on not only the roles of wife and mother, but I took on the role of his healer and primary support person. I ignored my own pain and suffering, I ignored the retraumatizing

effect working through his offense was having on me. I shoved it down—it didn't matter as long as I helped him get better.

I can tell you now, though. I was wrong. I was so wrong, and yet I'm now able to look back and be immensely grateful for that lesson and that growth. I have learned how to change my mind and live with the unknown. I can say I no longer am OK with something in my life and walk away from it. It's truly liberating.

The truth is no one will heal or change until they are ready to do so. No amount of support, therapy, or treatment will help until the desire to change comes from deep within oneself. Healing from a place of obligation to the legal system or to a partner doesn't last because it's not coming from an honest desire to change. True change, true evolution of a person, comes only from deep within oneself. Choosing to seek out the support to release the chains and burdens that they alone are ready to be done carrying.

Charlie wasn't ready to heal his demons. As much as I wanted to believe that he was, or that he could, he just wasn't. The amount of pain he was carrying was too much for him to face. Taking responsibility for his actions was not something he was willing or able to do, and so I had to eventually see that in order to keep myself safe, and my children safe, I had to step away.

Children come out of the womb and are regulated by their mother. Their temperature, heartbeat, breath—everything calms when placed on mama's chest.

As they grow, they begin to get more of that regulation from their environment but there is still a big part of them that stays connected to that initial place.

I didn't need to make sure my kids were OK so I could be OK. *I had to make sure I was OK so my kids would be OK.*

I was entirely backwards in who had to be taken care of first. Putting me first, and standing up for MY truth, turned out to be the least selfish thing I had ever done for them. By putting myself first, I actually created safety and security for ALL of us. And from there I was able to focus on healing my own shadows.

My message to the world is really quite simple. The only person who can change your life is you. Every single person has the power to choose differently.

Every single person has the power to create safety, security, and to find connection to those who want to support you. Once you have those things, the impact you can make on the world only amplifies. By acting from the space within ourselves, it allows us to speak our truth freely and we start to magnetize others who need to hear our message and our stories.

But first you must trust. Trust yourself. Trust that you can make that kind of impact on your own life. Trust that you can create a new reality. Trust that you are exactly who and what you have been searching for.

There is no one else coming to save you, but you.

So what are you waiting for?

Epilogue

The boys and I left Colorado in September of 2021, and together we have created a reality that I never thought I could have. I now have a new husband, giving my boys a new stepdad, a new home, and amazing new friends who support me in ways I'm still learning to accept.

I've created a business to support my passion for self-realization, healing, expansion, and exploration. Reaching out into the world and offering a hand to those struggling, still in the muck like I used to be. I share my stories, and awareness with the goal to inspire others to create their own new realities, possibilities, and magic. I believe that everyone has access to universal information, but first they must believe and find trust in themselves.

One of my big life dreams is to live in a world where trauma is more understood and those who need to find safety from their abuser or their child's abuser are more easily able to do so.

I now focus my time on the things that matter to me. My family, soul-fulfilling work, adventure, and play. And yes, there are days I still get frustrated with my children—any parent does. But I see them in such a different light than I used to.

Our children are our greatest teachers. They show us where we are keeping our own shadows buried. They aren't intentionally manipulative or combative, but they do show you where you aren't showing up like you know you need to be, and where you're actually focusing your time and energy.

My children showed me where I was hiding, and where I was choosing not to see what was right in front of me. They gave me purpose when fighting for myself

wasn't enough.

And for them, and for everyone who helped me through, I will be forever grateful.

References

Newspaper Articles

https://www.durangoherald.com/articles/more-suspects-arrested-in-child-sex-sting/

https://www.durangoherald.com/articles/formal-charges-filed-against-men-arrested-in-child-sex-sting/

https://www.durangoherald.com/articles/durango-man-pleads-guilty-in-child-sex-sting/

About the Author

Amanda Quick is an author, mother, wife, quantum energy healer, empowerment coach, speaker, and spiritual channel.

She lives with her new husband, and her three boys, living a life full of freedom, adventure and love.

Amanda has always loved working with people, solving complex puzzles, and helping others gain the tools they need to succeed.

One of her dreams is to start a non-profit helping others who are fighting for custody from their abusers or their children's abusers find safety in their current experience, and removing the financial barrier as a determinant of who wins and who looses.

Today she runs a healing and coaching business where she supports those who have been through trauma, find safety and connection to themselves and the universe.

Through her work she has opened up as a spiritual channel for new methodologies that combine quantum physics and spirituality bringing forward evolutionary ideas that work within the gravity of our consciousness to evolve and empower humanity.

When she's not writing or teaching, she's playing with energy, gravity and magic, or out enjoying nature and going on adventures with her family, mountain biking, rock climbing, hiking, and skiing.

To learn more about Amanda and other ways to support her work visit thesextraffickerswife.com.

GREEN HEART
LIVING
— PRESS —

Green Heart Living Press publishes inspirational books and stories of transformation, making the world a more loving and peaceful place, one book at a time. You can meet Green Heart authors on the Green Heart Living YouTube channel and the Green Heart Living Podcast.

www.greenheartliving.com

Made in the USA
Middletown, DE
10 February 2023